An Arizona Ranger: A Story Of The Southwestern Solitude

Albert Des Sulles

AN ARIZONA RANGER

A STORY OF THE SOUTHWESTERN SOLITUDE

BY

ALBERT DES SULLES

Illustrated by Hudson

BROADWAY PUBLISHING CO.

AT

835 BROADWAY, N. Y.

1906

(RECAP)

There he stood—murderer a dozen times.

To
Dr. Frederick Arnold Sweet
friend to all the miners and cowboys
in the gloom of the southwestern solitude.

t

An Arizona Ranger

CHAPTER I.

MY duties as city editor on the "Tombstone Epitaph" had brought me into disfavor several times with the rum-pickled element of the community. I am a peaceable man, and on entering my duties as editor of the "Epitaph," to show my confidence and good-will towards all the inhabitants of the camp, I discharged the shot-gun messenger and threw his boiler-plate turret out of the office. Things went along peacefully enough until the next election; then all kinds of business took a jump. Right during election week we had two lynchings, seven stage robberies and thirty-eight funerals, not counting Chinamen and Mexicans.

Now, just to keep business humming along in all lines, the editor of that dirty sheet, "The Bisbee Daily Digger," blew into my office and fired a salute of fourteen guns. I pulled the string on the dynamite keg, but she failed to explode. Four bullets lodged in my frameworks before I could drop through the floor into the bullet-proof cellar.

After drawing off the enemy my friends rushed for a doctor, who right skillfully dug out the lead and sewed me up. But the punctuation marks in my carcas are a constant reminder that this newspaper business is a very strenuous occupation, especially in this end of Arizona, where the climatic conditions have such a weird effect on the mind. The awful solititude of this vast, strange, desolate region of the great Southwest, brings out all the wild passions of man. The silence and sameness of this lonesome, dreary desert produces a madness, wild and reckless, which is apt to overcome the victim at any time.

Having fallen into disfavor in the camp on account of my inability to hit my adversary in five shots, I quietly moved to my ranch at La Osa, out on the desert, and here undisturbed by the neighbors who would like to sing my requiem, I have compiled a few notes which I hope will knock out that Eastern notion of Arizona being full of crooks, train robbers and cutthroats. Of course in a country like this it comes in handy once in a while to stretch the truth. Now and then you will have to take the law into your own hands and cover up your trail to look out for yourself, but the general tendency of the people is to obey the law, which of course you may try to interpret to your own convenience, sometimes, and in so doing you are very often justified.

To that splendid mounted police force, The Arizona Rangers, I owe my life, for when the enemy was gaining on me, as I fled through the streets of Tombstone, the bold Ranger stepped in and saved the day. As I slid through the cliffs and cañons of Bisbee, hotly pursued by the slandered citizen, the brave ranger stepped in and wrought my rescue. As I fairly flew across the desert, faintly touching the high places and making the mile-a-minute Jack-rabbit look slow, the dashing ranger lassoed my foaming pursuer and again saved me from a horrible death. So, therefore, while my wounds are healing, I will have enough to keep me busy in telling some of the adventures of those brave troopers and the characters who inhabit the mining camp, desert and ranch.

In digging up the history of some of the natives, I have gone back to my school-boy days when the camp was full of "cussedness" and the bark of a six-shooter could be heard at any hour of the day or night. Should any citizen take offence at my remarks in these notes, please settle with my bodyguard. He is paid for his diplomacy and shooting ability.

I lived in the camp of Tombstone, Arizona, a strange, wild region in the great Solitude of the Southwest, bordering the beautiful valley of the San Simon.

I attended school at the old adobe building, now used as a store-house by the Contention Mining Company. My teacher, Mr. Harry Smith, was a college-bred gentleman from Dartmouth. Firm and kind, brave as a lion and a bit of a sport, he was well liked and respected by the miners and cowboys.

Besides his school duties he performed the dangerous tasks of a deputy sheriff and justice of the peace. On Sundays, too, his melodious voice could be heard in the church choir. His services were always in demand as umpire in our athletic contests. Every pay day we "kids," as the miners called us, were in the habit of holding Burro races, which in that town were a big event, for the miner would wager his last dollar on his favorite. Excitement always ran very high.

Professor Smith acted as general manager of these events, while the stakeholder was an officer from Fort Huachuca, the government military post, about thirty miles away.

Our course lay through Allen Street; starting at the Palace saloon and running to the old monument down by the company corral. Next to a stage robbery or shooting scrape this race was the main event of the month. Unreasonable as it may seem, large sums were won and lost, on these events, by the cattlemen and miners.

Even the minister, or "Sky Pilot," as the miners called him, who held the important position of hoisting engineer at the old Grand Central Shaft, and on Sunday evenings preached to his flock at the "Red Light" dance hall which served the purpose of a church, would turn out to see the fun. "Heavenly Jim," as the miners called him, knew more about mechanics than theology. To him, if B.C. meant Before Christ, A.D. certainly meant After the Devil. But, he was a very eloquent speaker and ever ready to do a kind act or engage in a fight.

The story was told that he had killed a few toughs and then preached a very eloquent sermon at the funeral services, incidentally pointing out to his auditors the necessity of keeping on the right trail and throwing in a few remarks about how the bad man, who became fussy and tried to shoot up the town was in great danger of becoming the hero of a funeral.

I remember very well one bright afternoon in the autumn, at the end of the monthly pay day at the mines. A boy came to the school room door with a message for our school master to join a posse which was being made up in town to go out and capture or kill the road agents who had held up the Wells-Fargo express stage which ran between Tombstone and Fairbanks. Professor Harry dismissed the class in a hurry and lost no time in joining the posse which was at that time waiting in front of the Assay office, on the corner of Allen Street and Second Avenue.

"Turned your kids loose?" inquired the big sheriff in command. "Yes, sir, and now I am ready for business," replied the teacher. "Waal," replied the sheriff, "you and Kelly take the trail over to the San Pedro river. Keep an eye out for any transients at any of the ranches and notify the cow-punchers you meet, what has happened. If you see young Arnold, question him closely and if he fails to give the proper account, don't hestitate to put him in irons and bring him in. And mind, you don't give him a chance, as he is quick with a gun and quite willing to help out the graveyard cause."

"All right," replied Smith. "I will do the best I can," and digging his spurs into his horse's flanks he looped off, closely followed by his friend Kelly.

The two officers took their course down the

trail by the old Contention Mill, over the small
sand dumes, which sorely tried their horses, and
out by the "State of Maine" company's shaft and
workings; down the east side of the Mesa, to the
Charlestown mills and across the San Pedro
River, below the old deserted town. Here the
two men rested, ate a very frugal meal of Tortillas
and frijoles, the best food to be had at the "Cinco
De Mayo," the little Mexican hotel at the west
side of the river about one quarter of a mile south
of the ford.

It was not a lack of material or the poverty of
the proprietor that made food so scarce, but the
extreme laziness of the whole "outfit." The weary
traveler either ate there or not at all, but if one
wished he was at perfect liberty to go in to the
kitchen and cook the food to his own liking. This
was very seldom the case as the laziness around
that part of the desert was very contagious, and
the traveler preferred to postpone his meal until
he came to a ranch where the hired girl was a
Chinaman and the bill of fare more elaborate.

The news brought by the two officers did not
cause much excitement, and of course no one
knew anything and had not seen anyone for years
who looked like law-breakers. It would be rank
folly to know any thing in this instance. If they
told what they knew, it meant a trip to the county
seat at Tombstone; expenses while in town and
the ill-will of many good citizens back in the hills
and mining countries. If they knew nothing,
which was generally the answer handed to the
officer, they immediately reaped the reward of
their ignorance, in more officers to feed, more

supplies sold, and a general increase in all lines of business.

After finishing dinner and when the usual exchange of country gossip was gone through, the two officers led their horses out of the misquite brush corral over to the shade of four cottonwood trees, where another talk was held. After the council of war was over, and every man was strongly in favor of trailing the robbers according to their own plans, the two officers filled their canteens and following the advice of the hotel-keeper, struck off down the sandy trail which leads out across the desert and over into the Huachuca Mountains.

The shifting sand had filled in all traces of a road and though the two men had lived in the country for years, it was no easy matter to travel on the trackless desert after a terrific sand storm had just spent its fury. After riding for a few hours, it became very evident to Kelly, who knew the country like a book, that they were lost.

The horses were commencing to show the effects of hard travel and the now weary men tied them to a tall cactus and built a big pile of sage-brush near, so that should they come that way again, they would at least know the place and be able to take a different direction each time they sallied forth. It is very strange, but a fact, that people lost on the desert always travel in a small circle and keep wandering until they fall from the effects of thirst.

Smith wrote a short note, pinned it on the saddle, and after throwing off all their surplus clothing, struck out again over the sandy waste to

make a last attempt to find the watering place
known as Tyson's wells. This was merely a
brakish watertank in the desert. During the
rainy season, which came about once in five years,
this was fair drinking water for cattle.

The forlorn scouts wandered about, now sure
they could see a small town which immediately
changed into a large ship or beautiful farm, with
trees, buildings, and lovely inviting scenery. "I
see a town in the distance about five miles away,
I guess," said Kelly to his friend, who had been
leading the way. "Yes," replied Smith, "and I
guess that's the town we won't bother just yet.

"You see, I have been lost before, and when
towns begin to appear, and ships float by on the
beautiful ocean, it is about time to begin to pray,
if you know how. It is now five fifteen by my
watch and we have been traveling since noon.
We cannot be more than ten miles from the wood
trail which the Mexican wood haulers travel on
their trips from the mountains to the mines in
Tombstone and Bisbee. The best we can do is to
wait until dark then we will not be bothered with
the mirage and we may be able to see the lights
of the fort in the Hauchucas. I have a little
water left and I think we can hold out until morning.

"There is no use in walking around and using
up all our strength. We may meet some one, but
that is not very likely, as the 'round up' was
finished more than a month ago, and the cattle
and cowboys are all up in the foot-hills and
mountains."

Both men were in favor of waiting until dark,

for as Kelly said, the sand was so hot on his bare feet that he was afraid his corns would pop.

It was finally decided to rest and wait until night, as travel on the desert in the clear bright moonlight was much easier than in the fierce rays of the noonday sun. After resting a few hours in the shade of a misquite bush, and darkness coming on, the wanderers were about to continue their search for water when Smith called his partner's attention to a strange noise.

They listened and presently it was repeated. Kelly said it was his horse neighing, and they walked rapidly forward in the direction of the noise. Smith called out at the top of his voice, in imitation of the Indian scouts at the government military post of Fort Huachuca. At first his call was in vain, but a repetition brought an answer from some cacti close by.

On following closely the direction of the noise, which Kelly said was his Indian pony neighing for water, they came upon their own saddle horses tied to the cactus where they had left them early in the day.

This would have been enough to cause almost any man to wish some one would come along and fill him full of lead. To give up is the worst thing any man can do when lost in the desert. To Smith, who took life as a huge joke, it did not appear to be a very grave situation in which to be placed.

Kelly well knew that he would be the target for many a joke if he ever got back to Tombstone alive. In these parts it is only a tenderfoot who will venture out on the desert in a sand storm. Their situation now was certainly desperate. It was decided to turn the horses loose, first putting the saddles high up in misquite trees, where they would be out of reach of the coyotes, and follow them in the hope that they would lead the way to water.

The horses started off at a very slow gait, which Kelly said meant that they need not expect to find water nearer than ten miles; as horses turned loose will not become bewildered on the desert if they have ever passed that way before. After walking about three hours, it was plainly noticeable that the animals had quickened their pace, to which the two weary scouts were not able to respond, having suffered so much from thirst that their mouths and tongues were so swollen they could hardly speak.

The horses were nearly out of their range of vision though the night was exceptionally clear. Kelly, who was the more experienced of the two in the art of scouting, said he believed the horses were running, which meant water was certainly near.

Though hardly able to speak, Kelly had the most strength left. Smith, with great courage and never complaining, was struggling on manfully, but every moment falling farther behind. Kelly, whose occupation fitted him for such trying circumstances, had still much strength left, and returning to his companion, tried to assist him on, as it was very evident that according to the movement of the horses, water could not be far away, for Kelly as he turned back, noticed that they had stopped.

Smith was now completely played out and could
not stand alone. He pleaded with his partner to
leave him and save himself, which Kelly would
not do. Cautioning him not to move, for when
one is near death from thirst, the strength for a
moment returns and the unlucky traveler is very
apt to wander about and become separated from
his friends, Kelly hurried on and though very
weak and tired, he presently came up with his
horses, which had at last found the salty mud-hole
which bore the name of Tyson's wells.

The horses had waded belly-deep into the tank,
which was already half filled with the carcasses of
dead steers, while here and there on the bank lay
the skeletons of two prospectors, one of whom
had not been dead long and whom Kelly recognized as one of a party who had left Tombstone
a few weeks before to prospect in the Hauchuca
Mountains. Kelly knew too well that to drink
much water, even of the purest, would mean certain death. He only moistened his lips, bathed
his hands and face and though the place smelled
like a tanyard, he experienced great relief. He
always said that drink out on the desert was the
sweetest he ever had in his life.

The water had reduced the swelling of his
mouth and tongue, and after a short rest he filled
an old canteen, taken from the body of one of the
dead prospectors, with the thick greenish, slimy
water, and hurried back to his companion who
was now quite delirious. Kelly moistened his lips
and bathed his hands and face. This soon caused
the swelling to disappear and in a few hours
Smith, though unable to walk, was again rational.

He was able to talk though his tongue was cracked and yet slightly swollen.

Kelly knew that to spend another day on the desert meant sure death; so as soon as Smith could walk, he led him up the trail to the tank and his thirst, being gradually satisfied, there was no danger of his drinking too much water. After a few hours' rest, Kelly, who was the stronger, filled two canteens which he borrowed from the dead, then the two men started out again to try to reach "Soldiers' Gardens," at the foot of the Huachucas, eleven miles away.

This was their only chance as Kelley, who had traveled that way before, felt sure he was headed in the right direction. They struggled on, sorely missing their horses, who had died in the tank from drinking too much water. As they were beginning to despair they caught sight of the white adobe buildings on the very edge of the desert that were used by the soldiers on duty at the government gardens.

The sun had risen and was beating down fiercely on the burning sandy desert, and no human being in their exhausted condition could endure its fierce heat much longer. They were taken in charge by the fort doctor, who happened to be at the garden that day. In a few days they were ready to take up the march again, Kelly to continue the search and Smith to his home, as he had not the endurance required to travel on the desert in the fierce autumn heat.

Kelly had served many years in the Mexican frontier as an army scout. He was a man of great endurance and his knowledge of the country, his ability to speak Spanish as well as English, made his services quite valuable when some enterprising citizen made a forced loan on the treasure box of the Wells-Fargo Express Co.'s stage in some lonely place on the frontier. His love for whiskey had won him a discharge from the government service and the army surgeon at the Post claimed that rattlesnakes, hydrophobia, skunks, gila monsters and tarantulas had on different occasions stung and chewed on his well pickled anatomy, all dying in terrible agony. His love for mescal, the Mexican drink, which is a poor quality of wood alcohol, was something abnormal.

He was known to drink a tea made from misquite leaves and sage bush roots, a drink which is very powerful. Few men can drink it, and sometimes it has a serious effect on animals, for it was told, by a prospector in Hankin's trading place in Bisbee, that one night he and Kelly were camped in Ramsy Cañon in the Huachucas. Kelly built a fire and made a can full of his favorite tea, while his partner, Dutch Baker, went to shoot some game. While the tea was cooling, Kelly's favorite horse, munching around, drank the contents of the can, took one long breath, coughed twice, blew his insides out and fell dead. Though the champion drunk in these parts, Kelly never showed the effects of heavy drinking either in speech or movements.

CHAPTER II.

THE BISHOP'S CAMP.

AFTER seeing his partner placed aboard the
Post stage which was to take him back to Tombstone, Kelly paid his respects to the Post canteen,
quenched his thirst, mounted the horse which had
been supplied him by the colonel in command, and
looped off over the rough trail which led out
across the mesa through the chaparral up the dry
sandy wash, past "Nigger-head Butte" up into the
scrub oaks and along the rim of Montezuma
Cañon. Past the workings of the Ureka Mine
he went, and on over the summit of the exposed
reef, down the narrow dangerous trail on the
other side, not stopping until he came to the
settlement known as the "Donnelly Camp,"
a kind of a "go as you please" religious lay out
where each man had as many wives as he could
find work for.

The whole show was governed by one stud
horse comedian named Donnelly, who acted as
manager and High Priest over the whole colony.
He was a man of great personal influence and
magnetism. Besides recruiting his harem from
the great industrial centers of the eastern states,
he often persuaded the wives and daughters in
near-by towns to join his flock, but many a poor

soul lured from the east with promises was leading a life of degradation and slavery and would
be only to glad to escape, should the opportunity
present itself.

Arriving at the camp a few hours after
dark, Kelly found the place deserted and
quiet. Evidently all had retired or been locked
up for the night except the sore-eyed, stupid-
looking guard who paced slowly up and down in
front of the large gate at the south side of the
adobe enclosure. Kelly being well known to the
guard as an officer, was allowed to enter.

He went directly to the house of the bishop,
as he was called, and knocked on the door.
No answer. Presently he knocked again. This
time with more success, for he heard a voice inside bid him enter. Kelly pushed the door open
and entered the room.

A candle was still burning and in the bed, which
occupied all the end of the room, he saw the
bishop and his five wives. Kelly made known his
business, and told from whence he had come. On
being told that young Arnold had eaten supper
and fed his horse which bore signs of very hard
travel, at the bishop's house only an hour past and
had camped in the lower corral, Kelly decided to
wait until morning.

The bishop, who knew him well, regretted that
he was not one of the disciples of the church, that
he might loan him one of his wives. He gave
him permission to sleep outside the wall of the
white temple, it being against the rules to allow
a Gentile to enter the sacred enclosure.

Kelly with many thanks bade them "good

night," closed the door, walked out across the courtyard to the gate, where he gave the guard, who knew where Arnold was sleeping, strict orders to watch him that he might not become alarmed during the night and get away, as he wished to question him in the morning, and if need be, arrest him. Then he proceeded to the corral at the horse ranch just outside the walls of the White Temple; he turned his horse loose in the enclosure, climbed the hay-stack and being very tired was soon fast asleep.

Arnold, who had ridden very hard the last few days, arrived at the settlement in an exhausted condition. He told the bishop, who knew him, that he had ridden from Nogales and was on his way to Tombstone. After about six hours of refreshing sleep, he awoke, pulled on his riding boots, buckled on his six shooter and noiselessly slid down the hay-stack. He went to the corral, caught the best saddle horse in the group, saddled him and led him quietly down by the gate.

Arnold knew he was being watched, because from his bed on top of the hay-stack he had seen Kelly standing in the doorway of the bishop's harem. He knew that he would be arrested if he tried to depart, so he tied his horse in the corral, climbed the gate and walked slowly out to meet the guard who was pacing slowly up and down; now and then walking by the hay-stack to see that his charge was still there. To throw the Hickory Ruben clown off his guard, Arnold said he wished to get some water, as he felt very dry and feverish. The unsuspecting sentinel turned around to lead the way to the well.

Seeing his chance, young Arnold drawing his six-shooter, dealt him a blow over the head which brought him to the ground in a heap. Searching his clothes, he found the keys to the gate, opened it and led his horse out. Then he locked the gate, put the keys back where he found them, mounted his horse and quietly rode away up the trail over the summit, down the other side over the exposed reef, along the brink of Montezuma Cañon, down by the workings of the Ureka Mine, down through the scrub oak along the dry, sandy wash over the Mesa to the fort.

At the Post, where he was well known and respected by officers and men, as he was on all occasions gentlemanly and polite in his deportment, with winning ways and courteous manners, he had always found it easy to make friends. After eating a hearty meal, he mounted the horse, which he had borrowed from the settlement, bade his friends good-bye and rode down the trail out on the desert.

After riding a short distance, he stopped, retraced his steps, as he saw signs of a sand storm, and to venture out on the hot waste of burning sand under such conditions would not be wise. There was great danger of getting lost, and death from starvation and thirst must follow. The sand storm and mirage have been the cause of much misery and suffering here in this dreary, strange place, and it is not unknown in many other parts of the great Southwest.

Retracing his steps to within two miles of the fort, he turned off the trail near the Tower, where at night a light is kept burning by the Post

authorities, so that parties traveling over the
desert may take bearings from it. Striking out
over the country where the Buttes and foot-hills
break on the desert, he made his way across the
lava beds to the San Pedro River. On reaching
the river Arnold met with a party of Mexican
Vaqueros from the San Rafiel Ranch, driving a
herd of saddle horses to the range south of the
Barbacoma.

He traded the horse, which he had "borrowed," for one of the herd, bade the
stockmen "Adios" and continued his way down
the dry river bed past the ruins of the old mission
where he struck the stage road which he followed
across the narrow stretch of desert, up the hills
past the Schieffelin Monument and on into Tombstone. On the way he met a wandering miner, a
crusader with the curse of God on his back—a
roll of blankets—hiking over the trail. Riding
quietly up the main street, covered with alkali
dust, and people knowing he was suspected of the
stage robbery, his presence in town caused a little
excitement. Everybody supposed that he was by
this time safe from pursuit across the line in Mexico.

After stabling his horse at Montgomery's he
quietly walked up Allen Street to the Can-Can
restaurant, meeting many people he knew, for he
was reared here in town where his father had
been judge. After eating a hearty meal for
which Hanniger, the proprietor, would take no
pay, having known his father, the judge, for years
and receiving many a favor from him, he hired
a room at the "Ranchmen's Rest," a hotel where

cattlemen and miners from the country around made their headquarters.

After shaking hands around with his friends, many of whom volunteered the information that he was suspected of stage robbery, he went to his room, cleaned up, dusted his clothes and then started down town to hear a little news and get a little information. Strolling slowly down the street, he came to the establishment of "Peg Leg," the bootblack, who generally knew everybody's business and all that was going on about town.

"Hello, Peg Leg," said Arnold, climbing into the chair, "what's the news?"

"Well, nothing much, but I guess you'll be throwed in for being mixed up in that 'hold up.'"

"I will."

"Guess you will," replied Peg as he busied himself blacking the dusty boots.

"That's very strange. Why doesn't the sheriff or some of his men come and get me?"

"'Lows they will dreckly."

"Well, I'll be round here somewhere. I won't be hard to catch."

"Now, don't raise any row, Kid. Just go quietly along."

"All right, 'Peg,' but say, why do you suppose they are always hounding me?"

"Don't know, but I have heard it said that the Mormons ruined your father by stealing his cattle, and then got what was left to you by fraud. Quite a 'wad' on the stage that was held up; guess it belonged to the Mormon bishop; claim you knew about who held him up. Course I don't know, but that's what a 'plug' told me anyhow.

Where you been? Looks as though you hiked a long ways?"

"Yes, I just rode in from Nogales, pretty long, dusty ride," replied Arnold.

Peg Leg, whose knowledge of affairs, nautical, were very meagre, always claimed that he lost his leg "Looping the Loop" with Dewey at Santiago. The shine finished, Peg Leg wound up with a few remarks on law. Young Arnold went directly to the home of Harry Smith, the professor, and deputy sheriff.

As he entered the garden, which was fenced in with Swaya polls and cottonwood limbs, he was met on the porch by the deputy, who had recovered from his experience on the desert.

"Good evening, lad! How are you? I've been looking for you these last three days. Where have you been?"

"Oh, just rode in from Nogales. I am pretty tired."

"All right, come inside. I want to talk with you."

Arnold followed the teacher into the adobe room, where they engaged in a quiet conversation.

"Well, Kid, how did you make out?" asked Smith.

"I got through all right, but that was the worst night I ever experienced—rain, thunder and lightning; the whole country was incessantly lit up, flash after flash, and then came thunder, the worst I ever experienced in this part of the country, mountain or desert. I hid the sack in the old abandoned workings of the 'Silver Bear.'

"I tied my horse to a scrub oak up back of the

Spray shaft; then I walked up the narrow trail
until I came to the shaft of the 'Silver Bear.'
This claim has not been worked for a year, so you
can imagine what trouble I had in climbing down
the rickety old ladders which in some places were
rotten and in many places the square sets and wall
plates had pushed in and nearly filled up the
shaft. I made my way down as far as the two
hundred level. Here I struck a match and with
a torch made out of some shavings which I whit-
tled off, I groped my way about the abandoned
stope until I came to the cave.

"When I came to the cave I had to go back,
whittle some more shavings and light my torch,
as it had gone out. Unthinkingly, I had set my
sack of gold down by the cave entrance, as it was
very heavy, but when I started back I wandered
about and could not find the way to the cave and
I believe I must have been lost more than an
hour, but, presently, I found it and much to my
relief, as I was greatly worried and about to give
up the search. I hid the money in a crevice in
the second chamber up at the top of the water-
fall. No one can get up there, much less find it.

"On retracing my steps I lost my light and having no more matches I had great difficulty in finding my way out to the shaft. When I did find it,
I was nearly two hours making my way to the
top. When I reached the top I was so played out
that I could not walk, but the fresh air was a great
relief to me.

"After resting I made my way down the trail
until I came to where my horse was tied. I un-
tied and led him down the trail, over the hill to

the mesa at Don Louis. Here I watered him
and rode off toward the Huachucas, which I
reached about morning. When I reached the
mountain I made my way to Southerland's Ranch
where I ate breakfast and slept four hours.

"After my nap I saddled up, rode over the
mountain to the west side and along up the trail
to the Donnelly camp, which I reached greatly
exhausted. I slept at the camp for about two
hours, but the squeaking of the big gate awoke
me and presently from my bed on top of the hay-
stack, I saw my friend Kelly standing in the doorway of the bishop's house. Of course I surmised
what he was after, so about midnight I left the
place. I had to knock the sore-eyed gatekeeper
in the head, but as he was as thick-headed as a
pig, I think I did not hurt him much.

"After leaving the harem, I made my way
across country to this town, though on the
way I traded my borrowed horse for one out of a
Mexican herd. Then I had a horse of my own."

"Well, my lad, you have done well. The money
was really yours and I am going to see that you
enjoy it," replied Smith. "Now I have a warrant here for your arrest. I might as well serve
it as any one else. I guess you will get out all
right. I will make the arrest to-morrow morning, so you will have all day to get bail. It will
be easy for you to secure bondsmen."

"All right," replied Arnold, "I'll go to my room
to-night and bright and early to-morrow you can
clap me in jail."

The two friends parted and according to agree-
ment the arrest was made the next morning, caus-

ing quite a little commotion in town, as Arnold was well known and greatly respected. As the fall term of court was about to convene, Arnold had not long to wait. He was looked upon as a great personage in town, and as his manner was quiet and gentlemanly, he had many friends.

A man in these parts who holds up a train and gets clear is looked upon as a bold and skillful financier. To the ladies, he was a hero and to the men, a good fellow to let alone. Men stood around in groups discussing the case. They rehearsed all the "hold-ups" for the last twenty years; some saying this job looked like the work of the Earp boys, though no one was killed. Others laid it to the outlaw bands along the border, and held that the arrest of Arnold was a burning shame and no good would come of it.

Arnold had no trouble in getting bondsmen, as the thick-headed, ignorant sheriff was not very well liked by the miners, and they made no secret of their feelings.

There were many cases on the docket and the town was full of cattlemen, miners, farmers and jurors. Some of these were here as witnesses, while others, and the majority, were there as defendants. The mining companies were quarreling about the water question.

Most of the shafts here in Tombstone are down five hundred feet, but the Grand Central was six hundred feet deep and consequently had to pump most of the water and the other companies were not willing to pay any of the cost.

Men caught on this jury would not need to work any more if they handled the testimony

wisely. But on the last night before court convened the shaft house and buildings up at the
Grand Central took fire and were burned to the
ground, and despite the fact that guards were
employed to watch the property of the "Contention," "State of Maine" and "Grand Hog," the
buildings were also burned, one week later, causing the whole works to shut down, throwing many
men out of employment. As it was given out that
nothing would be done towards rebuilding until
the water question was settled, many men left
town. Some went to Mexico; others to Bisbee,
Pierce and the many camps around in the
Huachucas and Dragoon Mountains.

CHAPTER III.

THE TRIAL.

THE trouble between the mine owners and many cases of importance to be tried caused much excitement. Arnold was sitting on the adobe wall in the grove in front of the court house on the first day court convened. Around were men under indictment, jurors, officers and the usual run of town loafers who generally drop in at such times to pick up a little gossip and help run the government.

At 9.15 sharp, the court crier, Mr. Allie Howell, a lad who never believed in hard work, because he claimed it was folly for a man born and brought up in Tombstone on top of a gold mine, the richest in the world, to get out and work. He generally waited until some one with any easy job came along and hired him. He appeared at the court-house door with the usual announcement that trouble was about to begin. "Hear ye! Hear ye! Hear ye! The court for the First Judicial District in and for the County of Cochise is now in session."

This announcement put an end to all argument on the outside, causing the small groups of cattlemen and miners, jurors and defendants to drag their way lazily into the court house and up the winding stairs to the court room.

The first case on trial was selling liquor to an Indian. The defendant received a sentence of two years, though he stoutly protested that he could not keep himself supplied with "fire water," not speaking of having some to give away.

Gradually the number of cases on the docket were disposed of until case 1278, the Territory vs. Albert Arnold, Stage Robbery, was called. Although he had been indicted by a jury of his own neighbors he felt very little worry as to the verdict a jury would bring against him, as his lawyer knew how to select jurors.

Nearly a whole day was taken selecting the jurors. Some knew too much, others not quite enough, but eventually a full panel of twelve was selected. The taking of testimony took up the better part of three days. Many witnesses were examined on both sides. The truth was pulled and twisted around to help out the testimony of each witness in a wonderful manner.

From the prisoner's point of view he was an angel, and hear the witness for the prosecution tell it, he was a full-blooded, shell-back, green-livered devil and should be hung immediately.

The Mormon Elder claimed the Prophet had in his sleep visited him and told who robbed him. Furthermore, according to Divine revelation as he claimed, he had seen young Arnold riding out on the desert near where the hold-up occurred, behind a team of bay horses which he said looked exactly alike, especially the horse on the left side.

The taking of testimony continued all the day,

and about three in the afternoon the jurors were
given five minutes' recess. On entering the court
room again, a question was raised as to the number of jurors present. The bailiff started to make
the count. "The two Hogans is one, 'McCarthy
the Rat,' two; Mickey the Mouse,' three; Coal
Oil Jim,' four; 'Rawhide Ned,' five; 'Mike Doyle,'
six; 'Dish-rag George,' seven; 'Cottonwood,'
eight; 'Tombstone Frank,' nine; Sir Harry Hicks,
'The Englishman,' ten; 'Dutch Joe,' eleven. One
absent, Your Honor."

"Count again," replied the judge.

This time instead of starting with "The two
Hogans, is one," he commenced, "Red" Hogan,
one; "Shorty" Hogan, two, and so on down the
line; this time getting the required number,
twelve.

After the usual preliminaries of fidgiting and
shuffling around, the jurors all were quietly
seated. The judge rapped for order and the taking of testimony continued. At four o'clock, or
a little later, the evidence for both sides being all
in, the jury instructed, they filed out into the ante-
room, there to be locked up and closely guarded
until they decided on the verdict.

"Coal Oil Jim" was elected foreman, and on the
second ballot. After the count had been made
about a dozen times it was found that all had
voted "not guilty." Whereon, Sir Harry Hicks,
who had been elected clerk, wrote out the verdict which the foreman, "Coal Oil Jim," was to
read to the judge from the jury box. "Old Bill"
Richardson, the bailiff, who has lived in these
parts for years, formed his charges in line and

marched them into the court room as proudly as
though it was Napoleon's army and he in command.

The jurors filed into the box and when all was
quiet the judge called for order and asked the
usual, "Gentlemen of the jury, what is your verdict?" "Coal Oil Jim," taken a little suddenly,
climbed to his feet, jammed his hand into his coat
pocket, then with a look of dismay began searching his clothes to find the lost paper.   Unable to
find the document, and thinking a ready-made
article just as good, he stood erect and drawled
out in that quaint intonation which one often
hears in these parts, "Yer Onah, me and mah
feller citizens haave come taew ther decision thaat
this heah boy shed be turned loose."

But just as he had finished, Sir Harry Hicks
had written another verdict, an exact copy of the
first, which he handed to him, at the same time
giving him a kick in the shins which nearly
knocked him down.   "Coal Oil Jim" cleared his
throat for another effort.   Throwing his shoulders back, his head forward, and standing on one
leg, he read in his usual tone, "We, the jury, find
the defendant 'not guilty.' "

"Gentlemen of the jury, is this your verdict?"
asked the judge.

And upon receiving the usual replies of "Yes,
sir, it is."

"Yes, sir."

"Ee Heh."

"Si, Señor."

"It is."

"Wall I low."

"I recken."

Five nodded their heads.

"The defendant is discharged and the jurors who sat on this case are excused until to-morrow morning at nine o'clock," said the judge.

Arnold, who had been sitting quietly by the side of his lawyer, arose, shook hands with each juror and immediately left the court room with his friend, Professor Harry Smith. As they were walking along Toughnut Street they met "Peg Leg," the bootblack, who stopped, exclaiming, "By the scalp of Geronimo! Kid, you'd better duck your brain box out of sight or you'll get it knocked off, Kelly's looking for you."

With this he wheeled around and stumped along the bare stoney street to the yards of the Blinn Lumber Company. Arnold and his friend continued down the street wondering what was the best way to handle Kelly when they met him. They sat on the curbing in front of the office of the Bunker Hill Mining Company and directly opposite the Can-Can restaurant, quietly talking over the situation, when to their surprise they saw the dusty and beragled form of Kelly coming out of the restaurant.

He saw them at the same time and walking across the street shook hands with Smith and glowered at Arnold. "How you feeling, Smith?" asked Kelly.

"Oh, finely."

"Why don't you put this young devil in jail?"

"Why, he has been in jail, or under bonds to appear, rather," replied Smith.

"Why, yes, I heard he was turned loose, but

then he stole a 'hoss' and hit a man on the head with his gun, out in the mountains, at the Donnelly Camp. Have to arrest him again."

"Have you a warrant?"

"No, but the Bishop will swear one 'agin' him directly," replied Kelly.

"Well, wait until they do before you hunt any trouble. You don't know whether or not Arnold was at the camp that night. The people there don't know him. He might have camped at the Fort or at Bailey's Ranch at the foot of the mountains on the other side."

"Yes, he might have done all those things, but I have my doubts, and I know that that young 'cuss' was at the ranch when I stopped there and I am going to do my best to send him to Yuma for a while for 'hoss' stealing," replied Kelly, who was very much wrought up, and said it was an outrage to be fooled by a young devil and he the oldest scout in the country.

Smith advised Kelly to let the matter drop and not persecute the boy, as he always bore a good reputation. Kelly, who felt deeply the disgrace of being lost on the desert, and fooled by a boy, promised to let the matter drop, as far as he personally was concerned, but he said he could see no good of having that "cussed devil" running loose. He shook hands with Smith, warned him against having "that devil" with him and started off up the street to inspect and test the quality of rum dispensed at the saloons.

"I guess he'll cool off and won't bother you any more," said Smith as he and Arnold walked down the street to Smith's home. Arriving at the house, they entered and engaged in quiet conversation.

"You see, I think there will not be much doing in the teacher's line around here for some time, as many families have moved away since the mines closed down and four schools have closed, leaving the teachers out of employment and I am included in the bunch. The best we can do is to go over to Bisbee, secure a position and watch our chance to draw that money out of your 'bank.'

"I can rent my place here and as I am pretty well acquainted with some of those bosses over there, I don't think it will be very hard to find employment. You can stay here with me until we get everything straightened out, then we will take the stage to Bisbee and go quietly to work, as people idle are apt to get into trouble."

Smith rented his house here in Tombstone, which town was rapidly becoming deserted, and two days later both men climbed into the stage for Bisbee, the busy little mining town thirty miles away. About six hundred men at that time worked in the mines there. As it was the best camp in the whole Warren Mining district for the wage-earner, it was not always easy to get work there.

The first night they stopped at the "Castle Rock Inn," up Tombstone Cañon, a short way from town. After waiting around town for a week, Arnold obtained work at the Portage Lake Mining Shaft No. 1. Being a good miner and willing to work, he was first started on a drift from the three hundred foot level and having for partners a "Cousin Jack," two "Tarriers," two "Square Heads," one "Fish" and one American. They worked three shifts of eight hours each.

Arnold had no trouble in getting along with his partners, as they were men who had traveled the world over, and, like almost all miners, they were continually on the go. The "Cousin Jack" had mined in Wales, Australia, the Klondyke and every state in the Union and nearly every camp of any importance in Mexico. The two "Tarriers," on comparing notes, found that they, too, had been in nearly every mining camp in the world. The "Square Heads" had not yet toured the world, but they had the route mapped out and the "Fish," as the Finlanders are called in these parts, had not as yet made his debut in the "hobo" touring society, but had great hopes of doing so soon.

"Jack" Carroll, the engineer at the hoisting works, was a genius in his line of business and a thirty-second degree "hobo," who had taken a boil-out at nearly every watertank in the country. Not that he would not work, nor was he given much to drink, but there was that longing to be on the move. He always had some new camp in view. A perfect gentleman, a good worker, strictly temperate, while at work, he was, but he had that fatal tendency which seems to be the great fault of so many men in the West, that restless spirit which is constantly seeking new fields of adventure.

Carroll could tell the name of every town, water tank and railroad siding west of the Mississippi River. He had been up before every judge in the west on charges of vagrancy. It was his great boast that he never in his life paid a railroad fare. He had traveled extensively and being a man of education, was a very interesting talker. He often boasted, too, that he could catch and swing under a train going twenty miles an hour.

Arnold thought it would be very lonesome at first, but when lunch time came, each miner had a glowing adventure to relate about some Gold Camp in a distant foreign land and the fortunes they had made in gold mining in Australia and the Klondyke. Many of these men had prospected in South American countries. Others had wandered from one end of Africa to the other, making small fortunes in the gold fields, only to lose it in the settlements in riotous living.

Arnold marveled and wondered at the tales told by these hardy miners and thought he had heard the most wonderful tales of adventures in foreign lands, but his eyes were opened to new conditions after he had made the acquaintance of old Dan Hankins, who ran a general supply store on Main Street, near Tombstone Cañon. Here the miners were wont to gather and spin yarns about the different prospecting trips they had made through Mexico, Australia and the Klondyke.

This place was a kind of general headquarters for the people of the whole country around. Cowboys would gather here and do some wild riding, make some of the best throws with the riata that ever happened and it was an easy trick to fore-foot the wildest maverick that ever roamed the Range.

Old prospectors made long trips across the desert, had been lost, captured by the Indians,

tied to the stake, escaped, found rich mines on
the desert, only to get lost in a stand storm and
be unable to find them again.   Miners gathered
there and sunk shafts, timbered up the loose
ground, run long drifts and cranked up the Sulli-
van, Ingersoll or Rand machines so fast that the
strongest windjammer in the world could not
stand the strain.   They put in ore bins, and, to a
stranger, just happened in, this place seemed to
be in great danger of being blown to atoms by the
heavy shots set off by the miners.   But as these
meetings seemed to be held more to develop lung
power than anything else, there was no danger.

All expeditions to prospect in old Mexico, the
Huachucas, the Chiricahuas and Dragoons had
their inception here.   Arnold met many men here
who knew him as a boy in Tombstone, and as
miners as a class are not very bashful, he soon became acquainted with many people of good standing in the community.

CHAPTER IV.

FAST FUSE.

Arnold and his partners worked on in the drift until they ran into a body of sulphide ore. Meeting with such favorable signs they were taken out of the drift and put to work sinking the shaft.

Arnold was put on the afternoon shift. With him were the two "Tarriers," the two "Square-Heads," Kline, the champion driller, Burt Warning, whom he had known in Tombstone, and Jack Carroll for an engineer. The men worked away patiently. Kline was shaft-boss, and everything went on smoothly. They had put in a good round of holes, Arnold and Kline staying in the bottom of the shaft to touch them off.

The rest of the men went on top in the bucket while Burt Warning stayed at the collar of the shaft to watch the bell rope that he might shout the right call to the engineer, should the bell fail to ring, as the shaft was over three hundred feet deep. Carroll stayed at the throttle ready to lower the bucket, which hung in the shaft about twenty feet above the men, and hoist them out at the given signal.

Warning was patiently waiting with one hand on the bell rope for the signal to be given. There

was a dance in town that night and he wanted to
go to his cabin and "shine up."

"Great God, Carroll, something's wrong in the
shaft !" shouted Warning as the loud report of a
heavy shot sounded from below. Warning
knew something was wrong, and running to the
engine house found a lantern, lit it and quickly
ran back to the collar of the shaft again, just as
another loud report rang out.

Slipping the lantern over his arm he reached
out, caught the inch and one-half cable and slid
down through the dust and powder smoke until
he came to the cage which had jammed in the
shaft twenty feet above the bottom. The cable
being wet and greasy, his strength had nearly
given out by the time he was within one hundred
feet of the bucket, and his hands were torn and
his legs bare from the steel rope. He held on
the best he could but was jammed into the cross
bar over the bucket with such force as to break
one ankle, and his head coming in contact with his
knees knocked all his front teeth out.

The globe of his lantern was broken, but he
still had a light. Suffering greatly with pain he
released a small timber which held the cage fast
and then reaching out he caught the bell-rope and
rang two bells, the signal to lower slowly. The
shaft was full of powder-smoke and dust, and
suffering great pain from his own injuries, when
the bucket reached the bottom, Warning groped
about in the dust and stifling smoke, with his dim
light.

In one corner of the shaft he found Kline laying under a big pile of rocks, his eyes shot out,

and both legs and arms broken. Arnold lay opposite him, shot full of rock and nearly dead.
Kline, half unconscious, was trying to work himself out from under the pile. Warning hung his
lantern on a broken piece of timber and started to
roll some of the largest rocks off of his friend.

He rolled a big boulder off his chest. This
brought great relief. Kline now began to kick
and flounder around as men in his condition will.

"For God's sake, lad, get out of here. There
are eight more shots to go yet. We are all shot
to hell and can't live anyway. Save yourself."

"I guess I can stand it if you can," replied
Warning, as he dragged the poor shattered form
to the bucket. He had no strength to lift the
wounded man into the cage so he gave the signal
for two slow bells, which meant lower slowly.

The cage on the bottom and the cable slackened
so that he was able to tip it over sideways. He
rolled the injured man in and climbed on top of
the cross bar and then gave the signal to hoist to
the surface.

When Warning reached the surface, willing
hands took the injured miner into the shaft
house, where he was laid on a pile of blankets to
await the arrival of a doctor from town. As
soon as the bucket was empty, Warning with
another miner climbed into the cage again and
shouted to the engineer to lower them to the bottom.

It seemed like the crazy act of mad men to go
into the shaft again, as there were eight shots yet
to go off. But the engineer had to obey orders,
so he lowered them to the bottom. They climbed

out, caught young Arnold by the arms and legs,
dumped him into the bucket, climbed up onto the
crossbar, and gave the signal to hoist to the surface.

The cage full of men had just cleared the
danger mark when five reports rang out from the
bottom of the shaft.

"We got out of there just in time," said Warning. "The way those rocks hit the bottom of this
old bucket I thought they would bury themselves
in my carcass."

The men were hauled swiftly to the top where
ready hands carried the limp form of Arnold to
the shaft house to await the arrival of the doctor
and a train to carry them to the hospital. Presently down the cañon they could see the company's freight wagon coming at full speed with
two physicians. On arriving at the shaft house
the doctors hurried to the wounded men. Kline's
case was pronounced hopeless. Young Arnold
might recover. They dressed the wounds the
best they could in the shaft house and then willing hands placed the two wounded men into the
freight wagon on mattresses.

They were taken to town and placed in the
company hospital, where their wounds were properly dressed and their broken limbs set. Kline
had both eyes blown out, his face shot full of
rock, and both arms and legs were broken.
Arnold fared better. The first shot threw him
into the corner and buried him with fine dirt and
rocks, though badly bruised, he recovered rapidly
and was out of danger in a few days, and was
able to tell how, as he and his partner were spit-

ting the fuse on the last of their respective shots, two loud reports rang out and they knew no more until they came to, in the hospital. Warning said he had cut the fuse and noticed some of it was not of the best quality, but his partners told him not to bother wasting time but go ahead. If it was a fast fuse, so much the better. They would be out of the way anyhow. But as Arnold said, "It was a rather fast fuse, and we have won a home in the hospital for a month or two."

The two injured miners recovered rapidly, and Kline was able to sit up in his wheel chair two months after the accident happened. Young Arnold fared better. He recovered rapidly and within three weeks was to be seen walking about town. Though very weak, he showed little sign of a man that had been through such a terrible ordeal. Burt Warning, who had proved himself a hero and a young man of great courage, was worshipped by the miners and townspeople. His brave act was rewarded.

A popular subscription was started among the miners and in mass meeting it was voted to give him a gold medal suitably inscribed, to show their appreciation of his manly qualities and bravery.

Subscriptions poured into the committee from mining camps in Rawlings, British Columbia, Butte, Montana, Utah and Colorado. A beautiful medal was purchased and at a meeting held in the opera house on School Hill it was presented to him. Old Dutch Baker, who made the presentation speech, said: "Though I have traveled the world over, I have never—I have never before

seen such heroism displayed by a young man in
the face of almost certain death."

Warning could not see what so much fuss was
being made for. He said: "It is nothing more
than any miner would do had he been in the same
position."

Harry Smith, on arriving in town, hired out
with an engineering party to go to Sonora in Old
Mexico and survey a mine in the Ajo Mountains
for Colonel Dunn, of Bisbee. On hearing of the
accident to his friend, he hurried back to the
States, and was happy to find his partner alive
and well, for the Ranger who brought the news
to his camp had been told by a cowboy from the
C bar X Ranch that the whole town of Bisbee
had been blown up by an explosion of the powder
magazine under Quality Hill. Only four miners
escaped alive.

In great distress, Smith hurried to Bisbee, and
much to his surprise found the town still standing. And imagine his surprise as riding up
Dixie Cañon, he met young Arnold mounted on a
big white mule, taking a ride for his health. He
stopped his horse, shaded his eyes with both
hands, leaned forward in the saddle and raising
himself shouted, "Is that you, Arnold?"

"Yes, that's the way to holler and frighten this
skittish mule of mine. Whom did you suppose
I was, a colonel of cavalry from the Mexican
army?" asked Arnold.

"Why, Arnold, I just came in to see if I could
identify you. I heard the whole camp had gone
skyward," said Smith, getting hurriedly down

from his horse and shaking hands with his friend.

"Yes, I had a close call and I guess there will be no more shaft work for me. Well, I have been out long enough. We might as well ride into town, put our horses in the corral and go to the cabin and have a little chat."

So saying the miners mounted and rode into town. As they dismounted at the corral gate, a grizzled old prospector with three burros heavily laden with provisions for his prospect up at the head of Dubacher Cañon, came slowly along. "Say, kid, ain't you the little boy what was pinted out to me to-day up near the trading post as being the fellow what was blown up in the shaft?"

"I don't know. I was in an accident last month, but I got off lightly."

"Well, you'd better go to farmin', kid, and let the mines alone. I am a terrible old prospector, been hea'h mo' than fifty years. I skulped Injuns afore you was born, been blowed up so high that I get tired coming back. Advise you to quit the mines, kid. Yes, quit an' don't be wasting yer time. Why, I am wo'th a cold million and can't live in a house. Don't know how to spend my money; just keep a hikin over the desert, proddin' these yah burros. Go home to civilization and be happy. Good bye. Go wan you cussed ornery divil; go wan. We won't get out of town to-night." And the old prospector punched and prodded his burros down the road and turned up Dubacher Cañon, where he camped for the night by Hector's Spring.

"Pretty good advise," said Smith as he turned

the saddle stock into the corral. "If I ever make a 'stake' in this country I will loose no time in getting back to Vermont to see the old folks on the farm. Folks don't know where I am, and wouldn't I like to walk in on them and have a visit with the old folk before they die. It is eleven years since I left home. Never wrote a line or let them know where I am. It's wrong and if everything goes right with me this year, I'll visit the old homestead in the fall."

"Yes, and I would advise you to sit right down and drop them a line to-night. Can't tell what's happened in eleven years," said Arnold.

"No, I'll wait until I have a little more of these world's good, but this kind of argument don't win any bread, so let's go to the cabin and lay plans for the future."

So saying they went to their cabin on "Quality" Hill, up back of the old Queen Shaft, and entering, Arnold busied himself getting supper. "I don't like this bachelor life," said he, as he swept the floor, which was covered with flour, potato peelings and old rubbish of all description. "It's cost me more to 'batch' than if I paid thirty dollars a month down at Otto's place.

"The first day I started in here I thought I would have a fine time. I made a pie that afternoon in four hours and it took me eleven days to gather tools enough to break into it, so I threw it out on the can pile. Jim Craig's burro came along and ate it. I had to pay a freighter one dollar and four bits to haul him away.

"I have not had a chance to go up to the 'Silver Bear' Shaft yet, but seeing you are here we

will go and remove my property as soon as I am
strong enough; as I hear the Queen Company
intend to put a force of men at work there in the
near future.

"Come in," shouted Arnold, in response to a
knock on the door, as he busied himself frying
the bacon and potatoes.

"Good evening, gentlemen," said the stranger,
throwing a quarter of bear meat on the floor by
the window. "My name is Murphy, an' I hear
you was blowed up. Like the way you acted.
Good stuff in you. Knowed yer father in Tombstone. Yer a man after me own heart. Here's
part of a bear I killed up in Juniper Flats. 'Lowed
I would tote down a piece for you, as I 'breshed'
by on my way to old Dan Hankins. He's a cused
old liar. I was in this country and dug the fust
ore out of the Queen mine seven years afore he
ever thought of the Warren mining district. I
chased old Geronimo all the way from the 'Great
Western' mine in the Dragoon out across the
desert over through 'Wild Horse' Cañon, down
'Bright Angel' trail and shot his 'hoss' out from
under him as he was turning up 'Brewery' Gulch.

"I'm the oldest prospector 'round these parts
by a long shot an' they all know it, too. I fit Injuns and Mexicans right where this town stands,
been all over Mexico, down on the fever coast and
that is the cussedest place on earth. The devil's
never been there an' I don't believe he will ever
honor them with a visit. No, boys, don't yez ever
go to Mexico fur it's full of mullfrogs, holy monsters, galigators, rockadiles, wild cats, pizen
snakes and other divilment above.

"Keep away! Keep away!

"Powerful good rifle you have there," said Murphy, taking from the rack a carabine and glancing along the barrel.

"This town is gaining, boys, and going to keep it up. Other companies will be in here directly and a man having some good claims can sell in a few years for a good sum. Come alive boys and get some good ground.

"Getting late, I must go down and see that old devil at the trading store. He's a liar and I was in this country before any white man ever swum the Mississippi River. 'Ever stray up as far as my range why drap in. Well, getting dark, but my eye is jest as sharp as an eagle. As I bresh by again some day I'll drap in.

"Good night," and with a bang he closed the door and shuffled off into the darkness.

"Pretty old timer in these parts, I guess," remarked Arnold as he picked up the broken pieces of dishes which had been knocked off of the shelf by the slamming of the door.

"Listen! What's that?"

"Oh, some cowboys announcing their arrival in town, I guess."

"Must be a big bunch in this time by the way they're shooting. It is getting lively," replied Smith, and they both rushed out of the door just in time to see flames bursting through the roof of the old Custom house.

"Shall we go down?" asked Arnold.

"No, I guess not. You are not very strong and you can watch the fire from here just as well."

"We'd better go back to the cabin. Whoever started that shooting forgot the count, as three shots here is always the signal for a fire by night. Though it would seem no one is inclined to let up the shooting until all the ammunition is exhausted. Well, let's go in and finish supper. They will have the fun of swearing at that fire without our aid." So saying they turned and went to the cabin again and finished their meal without interruption.

CHAPTER·V.

OLD DAN'S STORE.

AFTER supper, plans were made to go to the "Silver Bear" shaft and remove the treasure which Arnold had hidden there. Though he did not obtain the money honestly, according to the conventional ideas in more civilized parts, still his conscience did not trouble him very much on that score, for he felt that the money had been taken from him in the first place by bribery and fraud. If he deposited such a large sum of money in the bank either in Tombstone or Bisbee it might arouse suspicion, and would result in a long drawn lawsuit if the Bishop should happen to discover any heavy deposit to his credit in any of the banks.

But to leave the money in the old abandoned mine workings was also another great risk, as the ground was continually caving and it was very apt to be buried up. And also there was great danger of its being found by miners who might be put to work there at any time by the Queen management. So it was decided that as soon as Arnold felt thoroughly recovered from his injuries they would go and remove it to their cabin. Smith, whom Arnold trusted, would then deposit it in his name in the bank in Tucson.

This course being decided upon, and as it was
now late, they could hear the miners climbing
the rock trail up near the old Queen incline, coming from work.   At eleven o'clock they retired
for the night, Arnold sleeping on his cot, while
Smith used a "miner's mattress and spring bed,"
rolled up in his blankets on the floor.

Bright and early the next morning they awoke
and after breakfast locked up the cabin and
strolled down the trail to the "Council of Wise
Men," or, as it is locally known, "Old Hankin's"
store.   Smith and Arnold went in and quietly sat
in the corner on a bench.   There were a few men
in the room, but as it was early in the day, there
was good reason to believe that many hours would
not roll by before some long-winded orator would
have the center of the floor.   With only a few
auditors, the exhaust would be quite light, but as
the audience increased, a little more steam was
applied and by the time the place was filled everybody was talking as fast and loud as his endurance
would permit.

Arnold and his partner greatly enjoyed the
arguments and disputes of the miners.   Friendly
though they were, each man believed he should be
looked upon as an authority.   According to the
social code which obtained around these parts the
oldest miners and cattlemen were at liberty to
take the center of the floor at any time and in a
long-drawn harangue tell how they fought their
way through the wild Indian country; discovered
all the mines; killed all the Indians and outlaws,
built all the railroads and smelters, and in fact,

each orator held himself responsible for any improvement done in the last fifty years.

"Azurite Bill," one of the oldest prospectors in Arizona, and who was also a veteran of the Mexican War, entered the store just as a dispute arose over the way in which old Dan, the proprietor, received the injuries to his back which compelled him to move about in an invalid's chair. "Azurite Bill" was a man of few words and many a timid tenderfoot thought it a great treat to hear him discourse on the early days along the border and the trials and hardships of the first settlers.

On entering the store he surveyed the place with a keen steady glance of his eagle eyes, dragged a chair across the room to the door that he might keep an eye on the street and seated himself, resting his dusty boots on top of a barrel of oranges.

"Wa'al, I'm a powerful old-timer, and I was heah afore anyone else. Ole Murphy never thought of this country at that time. I fit Injuns out in the San Simon Valley long afore Gen'ral Miles or Crook ever saw the army."

"How did old Dan bust his self?"

"Wa'al, I ain't sure as to thet. I was down in the Gold country along the Yaqui River at the time, but I done hearn tell that he got kicked in the back by a government mule."

"You air all wrong now," spoke up "Frying Pan," another old-timer, who never missed a session of congress, as the meetings at Hankins were called. "I'll tell you how it happened, 'cause you see I'm the oldest old timer in these parts.

"It was like this: Old Hankins, at the battle

of Lake Lagoona, was in command of the gun-
boat 'Mucha Grande.' They fit and fit. It looked
as though the Americans would win, but jest at
the turnin' pint a big case of canned beans which
was stored just abaft of the main smokestack,
exploded, wreckin' the whole outfit. It th'owed
the whole layout into the pond and if it hadn't a
been fur this yiah fish hound of mine they'd all
be at the bottom of the lake yet awaiting fur some
one to rescue 'em. Thet thare doggie of mine, his
name's Tige, swum out and drug the last cussed
one of 'em a shore.

"They all recognize in me their savior, and
what's more, I'm the oldest prospector 'round
these parts. Fust night I came here I camped in
Dixie Cañon. Volcano up at the further end was
boiling powerful smart them days. I camped
there that night and killed four Injuns. Next
mornin' I crossed over into Tombstone Cañon
and discovered these mines. I'm a terrible old
prospector. Whole mountains done got blowed
away and blowed back again and most all the
volcanoes done quieted down since I breshed into
these parts. I surveyed the International line for
the government."

"May the devil sweep hell with you and burn
the broom! Your the most low down liar in
these heah mountains or cañons."

"You'll rile me up to sech a pitch thet I'll be
tempted to break your fool head. 'Frying Pan,'
your always tryin' to stand on some one else's
reputation, and it don't do you any good 'cause
everybody 'round heah knows that Ole Murphy
was the fust white man in the whole Southwest.

I am the rile pussonage what laid out the Mexican line. I staked out the territory and built all
the canals, rivers and towns. My name's Murphy, an' I'm Irish. I'm the oldest prospector in
the world and I can whip the man that don't
think so." And with his shoulders thrown back
and his head up, Old Murphy strutted through
the store, not missing the chance to give "Frying
Pan's" dog a kick as he went out the back door.

"Now, looker hear," brawled old Dan Hankins,
"I want this heah disputen' stopped. This ain't
no camp meeting, and I ain't agoin' to be spil·ng
my trade in no sech manner."

Just as the proprietor of the store had finished
his warning, an old man known among the miners
as "Malachite Mike," rode up in front of the
store on a half starved wild looking bronco.
Throwing down a sack of rock, he shouted,
"Boys, look at that. Finest gold rock in the country. Me and my pardner just opened up a big
ledge of it. True fissure vein. Just been offered
fifty thousand, but I guess the man that gets it
will have to beat that figure just a little.

"Found it in the San Jose Mountains. Pardner
and I got the whole place staked out. I've just
rode in from camp to get some more 'grub' and
have that rock assayed. I hear people are staking
out claims all 'round hear. Wa'al, copper and
silver is going up every day and if that new Michigan company which bought Old Dutch Baker's
claims should prove a success, why the whole
country will sell like as if it was a gold mine
already developed. But their ain't nothing that

"I'm the oldest prospector in the world and I
can whip the man that don't think so."

can come up to this heah prospect of mine out in
the San Jose Mountains.

"Oh! never mind how I come to find it, I got it
all right and the ore is there. No danger of it
pinching out. As I rode in I passed a bunch of
cowboys down by the old custom house and they
told me about that accident at the Portage Lake
Shaft. Now, I've been mining and prospecting
all my life. I was in Leadville when that camp
opened up, and I haint ever saw a nicer piece of
work done than that kid did when he went back
on them shots and rescued his 'pardner.' I don't
know him by sight but I used to know his 'old
man' in Tombstone, when me an' him used to
work at the old Contention Shaft. I done hearn
they are taking up a subscription to get him a
gold medal.

"Well, now, if they should happen to bresh
'round my way I wouldn't mind throwing in a
few thousand to help the business along. I done
hearn, too, that old Jedge Arnold's son had a
'bresh' with the Mormons and lost out. I knowed
his father and a better friend never lived. I
wouldn't be surprised if the Mormons grabbed up
all the land and women in the Territory if they
are not corraled pretty soon.

"No, I hain't got time to get down; just scrape
them rocks together; chuck 'em into that sack and
hand it up heah. I m got to get 'round to the
assay office afore it closes. 'Sides if I figger on
getting back to camp afore dark I'll have to hurry.
Pretty hard to keep the trail out in them buttes an'
cañons by night, and this heah mount of mine
ain't none too tame.

"Wa'al! Adios !" and Malachite Mike rode
down the cañon to the Copper Queen assay office,
left his ore samples and continued his way to his
camp in the San Jose Mountains.

"That thar rock looked powerful anticipatin' to
me," said "Frying Pan," as he stretched himself
on the veranda and lazily rolled a cigarette.
" 'Malachite Mike' knows good rock when he sees
it, and I've done hearn tell them old Spanish
mines up from the old Mission was good producers in the early days.

"This old coon that comes into town on that big
white mule lives out there some'ers, I never could
find his camp, but he sells lots of gold dust down
at the assay office and though he has been 'shad-
dered' and watched like a feller watching for some
signs of a desert station when he's lost in a sand
storm, nobody ever was able to trail him any farther into the mountains than the old Spanish fort
at the entrance to 'Dos Cabezas' Cañon. If he
saw he was being watched he would camp until
night and then under cover of darkness he visited
the old Spanish gold mines, abandoned during the
fierce Indian wars which lasted in this region for
over sixty years.

"When the Indians were finally subdued, the
shafts and drifts had all caved in and brush and
trees growing up destroyed all traces of a mine.
An Indian who as a boy lived at the mission and
worked in the mines, was wounded during a fight
between the Indians and a troop of United States
colored cavalry. A colored trooper instead of
killing him when he found him, gave him some
water, bound up his wounds and let him go.

"I ain't ever heard what this coon's name is, but all I ever knowed him by was 'Nigger Ned.' He had a restaurant in Tombstone where the Can-Can is now; done a pretty good business; was a powerful nice nigger; never refused a man a meal and though his hide is black, he was the whitest man in the gold diggins and for a country like this heah Southwest. That's saying a great deal.

"But one day he closed out his restaurant, bought a prospectin' outfit and started for Mexico. No one ever saw him do any great amount of work in the mountains, but he brought in some fine gold ore and bars of bullion which had the Spanish mark and bore the date of 1832, showing that it had been stored away by the Spaniards during the early Indian troubles. Now, of course I'm not sure but I done been told that this heah Indian knew where the mines were and in gratitude to the nigger for his kindness when he was wounded in battle, showed him the trail leading to the mines up in the mountains above the old Mission. It's a hard, dangerous trail and though the nigger had been followed many times his secret has never been found out.

"'Malachite Mike' and this nigger have always been good friends and I wouldn't be surprised if the coon done showed him some good ground out in them mountains. The old Indian is now a chief in the Yacqui tribe and lives in the State of Sonora. Colonel Kosterlisca's men would like to get him as he was the leader of the last Yaqui war, but he is in hiding up in the Cananea Mountains and they will have a job to

catch him, as he knows the country, and though
he is very old, he still knows how to hide. The
American miners are still friendly with the
Yaquis and I think they will not give the Mexican
official much assistance. The old chief has many
maps and I believe if a fellow could get hold of a
few of them he could find some of the old Spanish
mines which gave up so much gold, but now are
vaguely known as lost mines.

"When I lived in Tucson, a long time ago, an
old Spanish priest came up from Hermosillo,
Mexico, and organized a party of fellers who
knew the country like a book. We left Tucson
at night, traveled down the Santa Cruz valley and
camped at 'La Osa' Ranch, about three miles from
the old Mission 'San Xavier Del Bac.'

"The old priest had with him many maps, crisp
and brown with age. These he carefully guarded.
After our day's rest at the ranch, we moved on to
the Mission and camped near the corral at the
point of the Mesa while the priest with his sec-
retary stayed at the little adobe in the cottonwood
grove with Father Armabisca, who was not only
priest among the Pima Indians, but farmer, car-
penter, teacher, doctor and lawyer as well.

"He looked after the interests of the poor Indian colony so well that they had horses, wagons
and many cattle and being well read in law the
American settlers found it very hard work to steal
the land belonging to the Pimas west of the Santa
Cruz River, as Father Armabisca was too well
read in Spanish law to allow the old scheme of
'land grant' to be worked on the poor Indians in
the courts of Tucson, as it had in every other part

of the country where a little bribery and more rascality was brought into use.

"Father Valmaceda had taught school at the Mission some forty years ago when the whole Santa Cruz valley was cultivated by the Pimas under the care of the Mission Fathers. There were a few left who remembered him and the next day while we were digging in an old adobe ruin, about fifty yards from the old church, we could see the Indians hurrying to the Mission.

"Father Valmaceda had spent many happy days there when the Pimas were wealthy and powerful. It had not occurred to him that the Americans had stolen nearly everything belonging to the poor Indians out in the rich valley and driven them back until all their land lay in a small strip adjoining the old church of San Xavier. Father Valmaceda could hardly go through the full services of the Mass, for as he looked out over the congregation, which forty years ago would have filled their old cathedral, he was deeply grieved at their forlorn appearance. The women were dressed in beautiful laces which they were taught to make by the Spanish Sisters of Mercy, whose school which once stood on the mesa back of the Mission, now lies crumbled and in ruins.

"But all was changed now. Even the old church itself which was once the finest in the land, showed the effect of toil and hardship of its congregation. The beautiful painting of the Virgin, at the right of the altar, which hung there for over three hundred years; the Savior on the cross at the center over the altar and with its an-

cient pictures and carvings, now sadly neglected
for want of money, gave the place an aspect of
sadness which greatly affected the good priest,
who, when he last stood on the altar, looked out
on a congregation of happy, well dressed, contented looking people, instead of a gathering of
poorly clad Indians who wore a continual frightened look and scowled on us Gringoes with a look
of hatred and deep suspicion.

"But presently, when we had dug about as
deep as the priest wanted us to, we saw the great
iron studded doors swing open. The worship-
pers came flocking out. Some stood in groups
talking in the light musical tones of the Pimas;
while others still chanted the 'Adeste Fidelis,'
taught them by the priest, Father Armabisca. I
expected the priest would come up to where we
were working, as my partner had already, under
the southeast wall, uncovered a small iron chest,
very heavy and strongly bound and studded with
iron braces.

"My partner wanted to steal this, but after what
I had heard and seen that morning, I could not
think of it and lest something would tempt me, I
called at the top of my voice to the priest who
was walking around among the Indians, shaking
hands and exchanging greetings with the older
ones, some of whom he had known when years
ago he had taught them in school at the Mission;
and stopping here and there to bestow his blessing
on a group of children who looked on him with
great reverence and awe.

"'Father Valmaceda, come here!' I shouted,
and at the sound of my voice every face in that

gathering was turned toward the hill. The
priest slowly ascended the mesa and on seeing
why I had called him, he thanked us and calling
two Indians bade them take the box to the adobe
house out in the cottonwood grove. He thanked
us again, paid us our wages and as we sat in the
cool adobe room, a young Yaqui Indian, who had
made the journey from Hermosillo with him, entered bearing in his arms a large bundle of maps
and charts. They were all written in Spanish
and as they pored over them, I could see some
marked 'San Jose,' 'San Rita,' 'Santa Cruz,' and
some others, whose names I can't remember.

"That Yacqui Indian is the same lad that was
befriended by 'Nigger Ned.' I saw him in Sonora
the last time I was down there prospecting, and
he took my rifle and ammunition away from me
though he paid me well for them.

"Our work being finished, we camped there
that night as it was too late to start for Tucson.
The same evening the priest, Father Valmaceda,
the Yacqui Indian and twelve Indian guides well
armed, left the Mission and took the trail down
the Santa Cruz valley by way of Ora Blanco to
Hermosillo, Mexico.

"I heard later from a feller who druv stage
'tween Nogales and Tucson that the party was
held up and robbed by Mexican outlaws near
Magdalena and three guards were killed. The
Indian boy got away with the papers and maps,
and hid them. Father Valmaceda returned to
Hermosillo where, worn out from the long journey and excitement, he soon died. The maps were
never recovered and try as they would the Mexi-

can soldiers never could catch Salcedo, the Yaqui
boy who afterwards became chief.

"Now, I've heard it said that the 'Nigger' and
old 'Malachite Mike' were great friends. Well,
I suppose that's where he got that sack of rock,
'cause it looks just like lots I've seen 'Nigger Ned'
bring in. If a fellow could get on the right side
of old 'Malachite Mike' he might show him some
good ground, but that's not very likely, as most
all these old prospectors are very secretive, and
being half loco anyway, they are very hard to get
any information from. But what I've said about
them maps is all a fact as I was there and know
what I'm speeching about. I've seen that Indian
and I know he is the same lad as was at the Mission and there will be a mine struck out in the
San Joe mountains yet that will put the whole
country on the stampede. I believe I'll just
quietly stroll down to the assay office and see what
that rock runs in gold and silver."

And "Frying Pan" struggled to his feet, rolled
another cigarette and strolled wearily down the
cañon to the assay office where he was very polite-
ly told that it was none of his business what the
rock assayed.

Arnold and Smith enjoyed immensely the
stories and harangues of the miners. They found
out also that to be in society in the mining country, a man must style himself a "Hard Rock
Miner." If a man is not in this class he is put
down as a "mucker" or just a plain "Pick and
shovel man."

In old Dan's store a "Hard Rock" miner has the
privilege of a front seat or he may take the center

of the floor in any argument, all others being
compelled to give way. Among the "Hard
Rock" men themselves precedence is given to the
oldest "old timer," and he is listened to with great
respect and reverence. Two boys, a Mexican and
an Irish lad, started to fight in front of the store.
Instantly there was a rush and the whole store
was emptied in short order style. After the fight
was over each man in the crowd carried his head
a little higher and there could be seen in the pos-
ture of many a decided tendency to strut, like a
rooster lightly stepping around after he had
whipped his enemy.

Arnold and Smith, instead of returning to the
store, climbed the hill to their cabin.

CHAPTER VI.

PROSPECTING IN THE SAN JOSE MOUNTAINS.

AFTER resting a few weeks, Arnold and Smith prepared an outfit to go prospecting in the San Jose mountains. Their outfit consisted of two saddle horses, two pack horses and five burros, to pack water casks on. They had been invited by old "Malachite Mike" to visit his camp in the San Jose mountains, and as it was now late in the fall game was very plentiful, and there would be plenty of water in the springs and tanks out in the desert and mountains, making travel very safe and easy.

Mining in Arizona and the state of Sonora, Mexico had received a great boom by the discovery of gold and copper and the influx of capital from the eastern and northern money centers, and a man having any kind of a mining claim could easily find a purchaser.

Arnold and Smith having been supplied by "Malachite Mike" with a map of the route to be taken to reach the San Jose mountains, felt little anxiety about the danger of crossing the narrow strip of desert lying between Bisbee and the Santa Catalina mountains in Mexico.

They rented their cabin to a miner, and bright and early the next morning, on the first of November, they rode slowly down the trail with their pack-horses well laden with necessities for the miner's camp. The first day's journey was uneventful. The aparejos being new and continually slipping, they stopped and camped for the night just west of the old custom house at the "Fonda blanco cabello." They put their pack-animals in the corral and ate supper with the many cattlemen and cowboys who made this place their headquarters.

Smith remarked on the slowness of the China-man who waited on table. He was a wise looking Mongolian who carried himself with an air of supreme indifference, and it was very doubtful if he could win a one hundred yards dash with a mud turtle. It was told by a cowboy at the ranch that the Chinaman had sprained his back herding snails when he was young and never recovered his speed.

Supper over, the men loafed around the veranda, telling stories, some writing letters, others discussing the condition of the range. A troop of cavalry from Fort Huachuca arrived and camped near the corral. They had been on an unsuccessful hunt for smugglers along the border.

Early the next morning the two prospectors saddled their animals and after having their outfit inspected at the custom house, they crossed the line into Mexico, following the trail which leads out over the great Mexican pampas and up into the San Jose mountains. The horses began to feel the weight of their packs and much time was lost by their continual slipping. Late in the afternoon they passed Skull mountain, a small mound out on the prairie which is covered with human bones.

Early in the history of the country the Spaniards invited a large band of Indians to the church, which is now in ruins, to make a treaty. As the building was not large enough to hold the people, they all repaired to a narrow cañon near by under the shade of some cottonwood trees. At a given signal the Spaniards began the terrible slaughter of the unarmed natives and not a man, woman or child was left of the poor unsuspecting savages.

The Spaniards paid dearly for their treachery, for a great uprising of the Indians drove them from their homes and many of their richest mines were abandoned. A terrible earthquake destroyed the mission buildings and prairie wolves scattered the bones of the poor Indians over the plains, causing old cattlemen and miners to claim that these mountains were haunted.

That night they camped at a small water tank on the plains. There was plenty of grass for the pack animals and though it was very dry, it made good feed. Arnold thought that darkness had come on earlier than usual, but this was accounted for by the presence of a great sand storm out on the desert. They had prepared their blankets for the night's bed and as they sat cross-legged drinking coffee, Smith noticed a light on the horizon away in the distance which he thought was a prairie fire up at the head of San Simon valley.

Through the gloom in the distance loomed the woodland, clear and cool far up the highland, where the timberline divided all the sand waste from the shade, and as the stars grew bright, the nightingale—lone songbird of the southern solitude—sang a requiem to the desert stillness.

The sky grew redder and a dull distant rumbling could be plainly heard. Their pack and saddle horses had quit feeding and walked around in a circle at the end of their ropes. "I don't know, lad," said Smith, "but I think that is a prairie fire. You notice how the sky grows brighter and that heavy rumbling noise becomes much plainer?"

"Yes, I see now what you mean," replied Arnold. "It is certainly a prairie fire and I can already feel the heat in the wind, which has increased in velocity since we made camp."

"You notice how restless our horses are? Well, that's a sure sign that there is trouble in that fire."

The light up the valley grew brighter, the wind hotter and increased in velocity. Occasionally a horse or cow from some herd farther up the valley would go walking rapidly by. Presently five cavalry horses minus their riders went galloping past. "That doesn't look very nice to me," said Arnold, who had been in a prairie fire before.

"Those cavalry horses belonged to that troop we met at the hotel last night. They left very early in the morning, going up the valley on a forced march. I suppose they were caught in the fire and those five horses that went by here are some that threw their riders and escaped from the troop."

The wind, now blowing a gale, was very hot, and it was decided to saddle up two of the fleetest horses, turn the rest loose, throw all their outfit into the shallow tank and prepare to ride for their lives. The heat was terrible. Great clouds of smoke and fire, mountains high, rolled down the San Simon valley. Herds of terrified cattle and horses galloped along before the flames. The clatter of hoofs and horns made a terrible roar. Arnold, who had been in a prairie fire before, knew exactly what to do. The cattle were terrified and ran with a reckless abandon, slamming into any object that stood in their path, so the prospectors were in great danger of being killed in the wild stampede.

Both men mounted their horses and prepared to run for their lives. A short way up the valley a great herd of cattle was thundering down on them. They could stay no longer. They shook hands and it was agreed if they should become separated and escape from their perilous position, to meet at the Mexican cavalry fort at the lower end of the valley.

Arnold lit a match and dropped it in the grass. Instantly a great wall of fire blazed up in front of them and swept on down the valley, they galloping on after it. When the fire up the valley reached the tank it would find nothing to burn and die out. Their only danger now was in the wild herds of cattle.

They rode on among the stampeded cattle in constant danger of being thrown and trampled to death. Still they could keep sight of each other as the fire lit up the heavens for miles. Arnold had the poorest mount and gradually was left behind. His horse was giving out. If he fell in that avalanche of hoofs and horns, he

would be trampled to death. If he straddled a
wild steer in that herd, he would soon be hooked
off and killed, so he gradually worked his way to
the outside of the herd and riding up beside of a
huge steer, he quickly straddled him and reaching around caught his tail and pulled it up over
his shoulder. With one hand grasping his
shaggy hair, his spurs dug deeply into his flanks
and the tail pulled up over his shoulder to be used
as a brace to keep him from going over the steer's
head in his wild plunges, young Arnold fairly
flew down the valley.

His steer plunged and leaped, but a good rider
in such a predicament is hard to shake off. Occasionally he passed by great heaps of dead cattle,
for wherever one cow or horse fell, others running along blindly behind would stumble against
them, fall, and be trampled to death. In this way
the old and weak were killed, making great piles
of carcases on the plains.

The fire behind having died out, the blaze ahead
sweeping furiously on followed by a dense cloud
of smoke left but little light in its wake and
Arnold found his steed was of uncomfortable
saddle stock, but he held on. His mount was
gradually falling behind. Most all the wild cattle
had gone on ahead.

The night now was very dark. His steer had
nearly given out, but he would turn occasionally to try and hook him off, though being barely
able to walk. As all danger had passed he could
make better headway on foot or perhaps secure
a fresh charger, so he slipped off his tired steed,
hid behind the stump of a cottonwood tree ready

to spring onto the back of the first horse that came along. He could occasionally hear the voices of cowboys as they rode along in the wake of the stampede to be ready at daybreak to round up their scattered herds.

He tried to shout but the stifling smoke had blistered his throat so he could scarcely whisper, and they passed on, but he watched his chance and as a burning stump near by lip up the vicinity he would have little difficulty in mounting a horse walking past. He stood on top of the stump and as a half dead looking bronco slowly moped by he quickly jumped on his back. Now a bronco is a bronco the world over and the poor animal, half frightened to death, gave one long snort, leaped into the air, turned end for end, humped up his back and threw the unlucky rider off into the darkness.

Arnold was stunned by the fall, but he soon revived and crawled back to his shelter at the cottonwood stump. He fell asleep and in his exhausted condition he slept soundly. Morning and daylight came. His sleep was broken by the toe of a boot rubbing into his ribs. He looked up and saw a tall young cowboy standing over him. "I'm San Simon Dick; excuse me for entering your bed-room unannounced, but I'm from the Mexican fort. A fellow came there last night to escape the fire and storm. His partner's horse was found outside the fort this morning, but the rider was missing.

"We all figured that you were dead, but I guess you will pull through all right. You take a pull

at this bottle and then climb onto that horse.
We'll go back to the fort and report."

"Well, San Simon Dick, I am powerful glad
to meet you," replied Arnold, extending his hand
in greeting. "I am a little stiff in the limbs after
my night's adventure. I'll walk around a bit and
limber up. You see my horse gave out and
Smith, my partner, left me. I climbed onto a big
wild steer and soon found myself solo. As my
mount didn't have much speed, I quit him at that
cottonwood tree. I watched my chance and from
my seat on the cottonwood limb I dropped down
on the back of a lazy looking bronco that was
moping by.

"The bronco leaped into the air, turned end for
end, switched up his back and shot me skyward.
I went up so high that I had a fine view of the
surrounding country. When I landed here, I
thought I would rest up a bit and was doing finely until you spoiled my nap."

Arnold felt very keenly the loss of their outfit. It was nearly all lost. Some was still in the
tank and it might be recovered if the place was not
full of dead cattle. "San Simon Dick" had informed him that no strange pack animals had
strayed into the fort, nor could any be purchased
there, not even a wild bronco. A very poor
pack animal as a wild bronco is, he is never thoroughly broken until you break his neck.

They rode on, double, passing many dead cattle
which had fallen from exhaustion. Arriving at
the fort, Arnold took a bath and enjoyed a good
refreshing sleep. The next morning they borrowed some horses and wagons, drove to the tank

and recovered some of their property. There were many dead cattle in the tank but they managed to recover two rifles, ten sacks of flour, slightly damaged, sugar, fifty pounds, salt, coffee, bacon, five pack saddles, cooking outfit, eight boxes of cartridges, clothing and two pairs of heavy riding boots.

There were no horses at the fort for sale, nor could any be purchased at the nearby ranches, continual Indian fights and raids along the border having cleaned them out. They could not return to the states as they must reach the mining camp with the supplies, or the miners would starve. So they bought six wild steers and broke them to the pack-saddle. Breaking a wild steer to the saddle is a very hard task and next to breaking a wild bronco it is the most strenuous occupation a man can indulge in.

San Simon Dick, the champion cowboy on the whole Barbacoma Range, agreed to help break the steers to saddle. The first day's work was very strenuous. The steers were driven in to the cavalry corral, then lassoed and dragged up to a post, the pack saddle put on and tightly sinched, then four sacks of sand were lashed in place so that Mr. Steer might become accustomed to carrying heavy loads.

Upon being turned loose, the poor terrified animals began to rear and plunge, fall over sideways and slam into the fence and walls, in a wild endeavor to free themselves from their loads. A few hours of this work and they were completely tired out. The sand was removed but the sinches were tightened to hold the saddles in place that the crazy animals might become accustomed to them.

That night the saddles were removed but bright and early the next morning Mr. Steer had to go through the same ordeal. In three days they were fairly well broken. The fourth day they were allowed to rest, while Arnold and Smith, with the aid of San Simon Dick, selected and bought many useful articles necessary for the journey at the fort store house.

Many of the provisions taken from the tank and vicinity, where they had been abandoned at the time of the fire were found to have been totally spoiled. He bought three hundred feet of rope, four hundred pounds of flour, ten cases of cartridges, a complete new outfit of bedding, as the last was destroyed, being unserviceable; four shovels, a saw, hammer, thirty pounds of nails; for "Malachite Mike" wanted these especially to repair some old ladders in the lower drifts and workings of the old abandoned mining shaft.

Early the next morning the steers were caught and saddled, and with some difficulty, for the day's rest had put the cussedness into them again. After much hauling and dragging around, they were finally saddled and the supplies packed on and lashed in place, the great corral doors swung open and the six steers went out on the burnt plain rearing and plunging, followed by the three mounted horsemen.

It soon became evident that the steers would not herd together, for no sooner had they reached the open plain than some started up the valley, others down; while two started into fighting each other.

They were all rounded up and tied together like ox teams. Tie two men together and set them adrift, one wants to go east while the other is headed north. It is the same way with cattle.

After much hauling and clubbing, cursing and shouting, the outfit made five miles the first day. "San Simon Dick," who had been hired to accompany the expedition, proved to be as good as his reputation in the cowboy line. The first night they camped at "clear water tanks," five miles from the Mexican fort, and fifty-two miles from their destination in the San Jose mountains. The day's work had taken some of the wild life out of the steers. They were watered and staked out, a fire was built and soon a good hot supper was ready. But just as they had spread the blanket and put the tin cups and plates in place, a wind sprang up, blowing sand into the potatoes and bacon and nearly blinding those around the camp-fire with dust.

The open prairie at its best makes a poor dining-room, but on a windy night when sand, dry cow manure and all other kinds of rubbish are mixed with your supper, it certainly makes one fierce for some plain grub. Around the campfire that night plans were made for the rest of the trip.

It was decided to follow the old abandoned mission trail, as that was much safer and easier than the dreary road across the desert. Game was very plentiful, though they might expect some trouble with the Mexicans and renegade Americans who infested the mountains. The first night out it was agreed that Arnold should stand guard the first five hours, while the rest slept. Then "San Simon Dick" was to finish the watch.

There was little to be feared from Mexican robbers, but all night long the wolves and coyotes would be busy trying to run away with everything in camp. Just as day was dawning "San Simon Dick" awoke and pulled on his riding boots. He knew he had overslept and wondered why Arnold had not called him. The steers and saddle-horses were resting quietly. Nothing in the camp had been disturbed except a saddle which the coyotes had dragged away and were busy chewing on the straps. Arnold's rifle lay on the ground near the fire and his hat was found twenty feet away.

Thoroughly alarmed, Smith was aroused and they both started on a hunt for their missing partner. The horses were quietly saddled and they rode over the surrounding range. They found the tracks of some horsemen, but so far from the fire that they gave them but little attention. Giving up in disgust they rode back to camp, and, to their great surprise, they saw Arnold sitting by the camp-fire awaiting their return.

It didn't take long to tell his adventure. "I was quietly smoking a cigarette when the first thing I knew a lasso settled over my neck and I was hauled out on the prairie, my clothes searched and when nothing was found, my captors demanded those maps of the mines at the mission in the San Jose mountains. Of course I had no maps and then they were in a great rage. They tied me onto a horse and started for the San Jose

mountains and I was quietly informed that if I
did not lead them to the camp of 'Malachite Mike'
and 'Nigger Ned' they would blow my head off.

"Well, we started out well enough by the desert
trail. The night was very dark and the sand was
blowing terribly and I saw right away that they
were not acquainted with the desert and by their
talk I believe they were miners. We rode very
fast. One fellow led my horse and by the way
he acted I believe he was stolen from the 'Turkey
Track' Ranch down the valley.

"We passed the big stone monument which
marks the grave of an Arizona Ranger, killed in
a fight with cattle thieves two years ago, so I
knew exactly where we were. My captors had
relaxed their vigilance. I was tied into the saddle, but I was determined to be true to my friend
'Malachite Mike,' and not divulge any secrets.
My hands were free and I watched my chance.
Reaching forward I slipped the bridle off my
horses's head and digging my spurs into his flanks
he leaped into the air with a terrified snort and
plunged off into the darkness.

"Taken by surprise my captors lost their heads
for a few seconds; time enough for me to be out
of range of the fusilade of bullets that flew after
me. My mount being a noble animal, fairly flew
down the valley. I had freed my legs and after
about one hour's ride down the trail, I saw the
light of the camp-fire. I knew the horse and saddle were stolen. Of course if the owner found
me with the outfit, he would shoot me full of holes
and then ask questions afterwards. My mount
had slackened his speed somewhat and when I

was opposite this light I slipped off behind and made my way to the camp and was in luck to find it our own outfit.

"Well, we will have to be careful, if those fellows are not lost on the desert, they will make their way to the mountains and if they ever catch me again, I will get combed with a club."

San Simon Dick, who had been locked up in almost every jail in Mexico and managed to escape, thought Arnold had done a stunt which when it reached the trading-post and ranch headquarters would outshine his best effort. So he resolved, if the chance came, to do something which would keep the cowboys, ranchmen and miners talking for many a day and cause them to bow and scrape when he "breshed" by.

CHAPTER VII.

TROUBLE ON THE TRAIL.

AFTER breakfast the steers were saddled; the supplies lashed in place and the expedition drew slowly away from camp. Two days' work had taken some of the wildness out of the steers so they went along quietly without being yoked together. But every animal, both human and brute, is subject to those wild crazy fits of reckless abandon, so noticeable in this strange desolate region of the great Southwest.

At night on the lonely desert you are seated lazily in the saddle slowly rolling a cigarette. The evening is calm. The herd bedded for the night. Everything is so quiet that you have no thought of a stampede.

Suddenly up leaps a crazy steer and with a terrified snort, head down, tail straight in the air, he bolts down off the valley, claiming full right of way and slamming into any object that may be in his path, the whole herd doing their best to overtake him. Your horse with the lamb-like disposition now does his level best to throw you. If he can't shoot you over his head, he will rear up and fall over backwards, and unless you are an expert rider you are likely to be crushed to death. The crazy spell is on and must run its course.

As the man who drinks out of the Hassiampa River with his head down stream is doomed forever after to be an eternal liar, so the poor unfortunate man or beast who is unlucky enough to inhale the essence of Loco weed is ever after troubled with that strange sickness, so prevalent in the arid regions, known as fool-in-the-head, or just plain "Loco."

The steers plodded slowly along, the packs, lashed securely under the watchful eye of "San Simon Dick," were held well in place and caused very little trouble by slipping or shifting. That night they camped at "Dripping Springs" ranch, owned by Colonel Bill Cornell, the cattle king of the Southwest, and the largest landowner in the territory. They received a royal welcome, for Arnold's father had been a great friend of the Colonel's in the prosperous days of Tombstone.

The Colonel generously offered them pack horses, but it was decided to continue with the steers. They were now well broken and as breaking broncos to carry a pack-saddle is no easy task, the generous offer was declined, for in this end of the country the horse has his say about the labor question. He believes in eight hours rest three times a day and three hundred and sixty-five days in the year. Should you try to break him of this notion he does his level best to break your neck. The pack animals were put in the corral for the night while the saddle stock were hobbled and turned out to graze.

There were many visitors at the ranch that night; a merry coaching party of army officers with their families from Fort Huachuca; Señior

Don Emilio Del Valle with his family from the
Hasciendo "San Ramon" in the Cananea mountains, State of Sonora, had just arrived to pay a
visit to the Americanos. Old "High Jolly," a
wandering gold hunter, arrived that day and always carrying his fiddle, he was ever a welcome
guest at the lonely ranch houses. The genial
landlord was a jolly good fellow and now at his
home was the liveliest crowd he had chanced to
meet in years.

The supper over, the spacious veranda was
cleared for a good old-fashioned cowboy dance,
much to the delight of the army ladies present, for
they were just from the east and had never enjoyed the wholesome fun of a ranch house cotillion.

Old "High Jolly," who played wholly by hand,
mounted a box in the corner with his trusty fiddle
and lost no time in sawing out the "Arkansas
Traveler," while "San Simon Dick's" · sonorous
voice could be heard above the noise of clanking
spurs and high-heeled boots scraping on the floor,
while he called out the dance in the most approved
cowboy style, as he whirled and flew through the
dance. A few verses of the original one hundred
and fifteen I remember as sung at the ranch that
night:

> Everybody came alive!!
> Douse your lights and catch your sage hens,
> Trade your hosses an' turn 'em roun',
> Watch your pardners and watch 'em close,
> When you come to 'em, double the dose,
> Wheel! Wheel! Wheel!

Everyone a dancin' an' go hog-wild.
Alaman hush an' th' elbow push
An' th' Arkansas wind.
Wheel!   Wheel!   Wheel!

Cross the desert now with you' gal,
Pace right along
An' treat her well,
Wheel!   Wheel!   Wheel!

Everyone a dancin' an' a swingin' roun',
Flyin' in the air an' a
Flyin' on th' groun',
Wheel!   Wheel!   Wheel!

Ketch you pardners an' trot in style.
Keep a pitchin' an' a prancin' all the while,
Drag 'em roun' like stormy weather,
Hoofs in th' air now keep together,
Wheel!   Wheel!   Wheel!

Fust hoss on th' right
Slide 'cross an' back,
Everyone a raggin',
Don't lose the track,
Wheel!   Wheel!   Wheel!

Keep a dancin' an' a prancin',
Now keep good form
Turnin' an' a swingin'
Like a big sand storm,
Rearin' an' a pitchin'
Like a wild mustang,
Wheel!   Wheel!   Wheel!

Down on you' feet an'
Drag you' spurs,
Scrape 'em hard an'
Make 'em rattle,
Keep a snortin' an' a
Tearin' like a bunch of cattle,
Wheel! Wheel! Wheel!

Rope you' pardners an'
Trot in fours,
We'll keep on dancin'
Fo' seventy hours.
Shake that gal an'
Grab another.
Keep on a dancin'
All together.
Wheel! Wheel! Wheel!

Fly in a circle,
Now break you' necks,
Everybody kill 'em self,
Do you best.
Swing fou' times,
Then all take a rest.
Wheel! Wheel! Wheel!

Pow'ful wild dance
An' a jolly good treat,
S'lute you' pardners
An' take you' seat.
Wheel! Wheel! Wheel!

And the merry dancers sought seats and par-
took of the refreshments served by the snail-

gaited Chinaman. Had "San Simon Dick" not
run out of breath he might be singing that song
yet. To the Eastern members of the party that
cowboy dance was a revelation and "San Simon
Dick" came in for great praise.

Late that night the party broke up, the guests
retiring to their rooms. Arnold and Smith
camped out near the corral, while "San Simon
Dick" took his turn at standing guard. The expected raid did not materialize and early the next
morning they left the ranch and after five hours'
travel they struck the trail which led up between
the cliffs and buttes to the mesa and table-lands
of the wild and dangerous San Jose mountains.

The trail up the broken wall of the mesa was
very narrow and winding. Arnold led the way,
mounted on his sturdy pony; the pack animals
following along in single file, for the trail here
was very narrow and dangerous. A misstep
would send one to the bottom of the cañon five
hundred feet below to certain death.

From the valley to the top of the mesa was but
half a mile in a direct line, but the narrow winding path was much longer, and great care was
necessary as the steers would break their hoofs on
the sharp rocks causing them to go lame and making them unfit for further service.

On reaching the level plain above it was decided
to make camp and rest, as the steers, not being
shod, would go lame if overworked. They were
now camped on the mesa, a high table-land which
extended from the San Jose mountains to the
great pampas in Mexico. It was noted as a great
hunting-ground, for the terrible raids of the

Yaqui Indians had scattered the great herds of horses and cattle, leaving the feeding ground for deer and antelope. The animals were securely staked out after being watered at the tank near by.

Arnold noticed tracks in the sand near the rim of the tank. He called "San Simon Dick," who examined them closely and after very close scrutiny he came to the conclusion that they were not over a day old. They returned to camp and it was resolved to keep a bright lookout that night. There might be no trouble, or no reason for feeling any alarm. But from past experiences Arnold felt that it would be wise to keep a careful guard posted.

Just before darkness began to settle over the camp, a large white horse was seen cautiously approaching the tank, followed by eight shaggy broncos. "San Simon Dick" quickly saddled up his horse and rode quietly around to the rear of the bunch, first giving instructions to Arnold to frighten the horses away from the tank before they had a drink.

The white leader was a noble looking animal, full of life and of powerful build. If "San Simon Dick" succeeded in catching him he would certainly prove his right to the title of "King of the cowboys." He rode slowly to the rear of the herd, lasso in hand, ready for a throw. Suddenly the leader becoming alarmed, wheeled quickly around and dashed off over tpe pampas. "San Simon Dick" mounted on one of the best saddle horses that ever left the turkey track ranch, felt sure he could catch the king of the drove. Digging his

spurs into the ribs of his charger, he fairly flew
over the pampas.

He had a good start and the king was hemmed
in. He would have to jump over the side of the
cliff or rely on his superior speed to effect his
escape. It was a desperate race and if the throw
was successful, he would have to use great cau-
tion, for the slightest mistake meant certain death.

As soon as he was near enough, he threw the
lasso over hand after the style effected by the
mountain cowboys. The throw was a very difficult one. The bronco tried to dodge, but the
trick was anticipated and he was caught by the
front feet, sent spinning into the air and landed
on his side in a clump of bushes, where he laid
motionless, the wind knocked out of him by the
fall.

Smith had already saddled his horse and upon
seeing the wild king caught, he hurried to the assistance of his comrade. Very skillfully throwing
his lasso over the bronco's head, he circled around
and pulled in the opposite direction, making it impossible for the horse to regain his feet after he
recovered from the shock caused by the terrible
fall.

The king of the pampas was still out of commission, and as any one who has ever engaged in
that gentle occupation of breaking broncos is very
well aware, this was the best time to put the saddle on and ride him. "San Simon Dick" was
king of the cowboys. He could ride bareback
the fiercest outlaw bronco that ever roamed the
Barba comera, "Turkey track," or the "Ville San
Simon" range. He had never tried his skill on

the wild mountain broncos that roam the high
mesa and mountain peaks of the San Jose and
Cananea mountains. He had won his title at the
cowboy carnival in Tucson by taking the first
prize three years in succession.

Here was a good chance for a little practice in
bare-back riding, so he slipped a hackamore over
the bronco's head, took the lassos off his neck and
forefeet, then stood quietly by waiting for the
prostrate animal to try and regain his feet. He
had not long to wait. The horse, dazed by the
fall, soon recovered, and as he struggled to his
feet the king of the bronco-busters leaped on his
back.

The thoroughly frightened bronco lost no time
in getting rid of his rider. With a loud snort he
leaped into the air, turned end for end, humped up
his back and shot the king of all cowboys up into
the clouds. The unfortunate rider came down
spread-eagle in a clump of sage brush, somewhat
dazed, but he recovered in time to see his con-
queror disappearing in the gloom.

"San Simon Dick" was very much downcast
over his mishap, but that was his first experience
with mountain horses and perhaps he would do
better the next time. The three men walked
slowly back to camp, Arnold leading the horses.
It was greatly regretted that the noble animal had
escaped, for the leader of a drove of wild horses
is always very much prized by the cowboys and
cattlemen, very much sought after and seldom
caught.

After supper the men rolled up in their blankets
very early, Smith taking his turn at guard duty.

The night was much cooler than any they had experienced in the valley and plains. At twelve
o'clock Arnold got up and finished the watch and
the dawn of day found the animals all saddled and
ready for the journey, for they had lost much
valuable time on account of the prairie fire and
the loss of their burros.

"Malachite Mike" would be uneasy. The country was infested with renegade Indians and train
robbers, who usually spend the heated term up in
the mountains where the air is cool and bracing.
They never overlook a chance to make a call loan
on the lonely prospectors who are returning from
"civilization" well laden with a new supply of
"grub."

They urged the pack-animals along. It was
fifteen miles across the mesa to "Dos Cabezas"
cañon. They could make that by sundown easily.
It would take two days to travel the ten miles of
trail up the cañon for the way was very steep and
rough and they would have to exercise great cau-
tion, as the steers began to show signs of sore
feet.

The trail in the cañon was extremely dangerous; a narrow shelf of rock scarcely wide enough
for horse and rider to pass safely. They made
good headway and at noon were half way across
the Mesa. The animals were beginning to show
signs of thirst, but there was no water nearer
than the tanks at the mouth of "Dos Cabezas"
cañon, known to the cowboys and prospectors as
"Troopers' Rest Springs."

The packs were slipping badly and a short halt
was made to adjust the aperejos and repair a

broken latigo. Game was very plentiful and
Arnold brought down a fine antelope with his
carabine at three hundred yards. A bunch of
wild horses appeared on the top of a butte away
up in the mountains, causing them to lay plans
for a grand horse round-up in the near future.

The pack train had emerged from the long
stretch of bunch grass and entered the thick
chaparral bordering the edge of the Mesa. The
steers had quickened their pace, perceiving that
water, which they were in great need of, was immediately ahead. The tanks being the objective
point, they required no herding.

Riding leisurely along, laughing and joking,
anticipating no trouble, the three prospectors
brought up the rear. Suddenly, out of the bushes
not fifteen feet away in the center of the trail,
arose a huge mountain bear. The terrified steers
bolted right and left, tails in the air, they fairly
flew over the prairie, scattering bedding and frying pans, potatoes and mining utensils all over
the pampas.

The lead steer seemed bound to reach Mexico
before sundown as he flew over the prairie, scattering his load of flour and other provisions all
over the country, leaving an irregular white trail
in his wake. Taken completely by surprise it was
some time before the men recovered their wits.
Arnold's horse had bolted at the first rush, nearly
unseating him, but he soon recovered and grasping his carabine he turned loose at the runaway
steers, ordering his comrades to follow suit.

Some of the pack animals were nearly out of
range but on the third shot the leader fell. Arnold

being armed with a high power government carabine, brought down four in twelve shots; good
marksmanship considering the fact that he was
shooting at a running object at long range and
mounted on a horse that behaved poorly under
fire. Smith, somewhat bewildered at first, did
not commence firing until the steers were well out
of range, but dismounted, and using the saddle
as a rest, he managed to bring down two out of
eleven shots.

At the first appearance of the bear, "San Simon
Dick's" horse reared up and fell over backwards,
throwing his rider off into the bushes. Unhorsed
and separated from his carabine he scrambled to
his feet just in time to dodge the huge brute as
it rushed at him. Drawing his six-shooter he
sent four bullets into its head as it turned to
charge again, killing it instantly. Two little
black cubs came running down the path, innocent
cause of all the trouble. Quickly tying them together, he mounted his horse and rode to the assistance of Arnold and Smith, who were busy
gathering up the scattered supplies.

After a hurried consultation, it was decided to
gather the scattered supplies into one pile and use
their saddle horses to pack them as far as the
tank at the mouth of the cañon where in three
days they could with the aid of "Malachite Mike"
and his two mules get them up to the mines.

Arnold had used good judgment in shooting
the steers. It would have been useless to try to
lasso them, so the only way to save the provisions
was to turn loose and shoot them down. They
worked faithfully and about midnight they had

everything transferred to the new camp at "Troopers' Rest" Springs. Being worn out and thoroughly exhausted they rolled into their blankets and were soon asleep, "San Simone Dick" taking his turn as guard.

Mountain lions, wild cats, bear and loger wolves kept the horses in a state of terror all night by their howling swauree held over the carcases of the dead steers. The little cubs, captured that day, gave no trouble and soon became as tame as kittens. Before sunup they were off up the trail; the three horses heavily loaded and "San Simon Dick" stopping behind as guard. In two days they returned reinforced by two big mules, and all the rest of the provisions were easily disposed of among the five pack animals.

They struck out for camp at a rapid pace, Arnold leading the van, for it was necessary to keep a sharp lookout for wild cattle along the narrow, dangerous trail where a misstep would send the unfortunate traveler to his death a thousand feet below in the wild unknown cañon bed. On arriving at the prospectors' camp, just below the old abandoned mission buildings, they were introduced all around after the style obtaining in the mines and cattle country, after which they held a grand levee.

They received great praise for the manner in which they had conducted the expedition into that wild, unexplored region, for the determination and faithfulness shown through all their hardships and trouble. So well was "Nigger Ned" and "Malachite Mike" satisfied with their work that they were al' employed permanently.

"San Simon Dick" as chief carjerdero or boss
packer, in charge of the supply train; Harry
Smith was to conduct the survey, while Arnold
looked after the purchasing of supplies and other
company business in Busbee.

The prospectors were greatly troubled when
told about the attempted capture of Arnold. All
were sworn to faithfulness and secrecy and each
one repaired to his post of duty. They had
struck a bonanza and all through the kindness,
honesty and ability of that rough looking, kind-
hearted old black man "Nigger Ned."

CHAPTER VIII.

THE DESERT STATION

THE three men, though sorely in need of rest, lost no time in returning to Bisbee to look after their different departments. A complete survey of the mines was necessary, for as soon as it became noised about that gold had been found, prospectors would flock in, eager to jump any claim that was not properly surveyed and recorded.

Though all the necessary ground was recorded in Tombstone in the name of John Edwards, or as he was more familiarly known, "Nigger Ned," he seldom mentioned his rich holdings to anyone. His quiet demeanor and gentlemanly ways won the respect of the haughty cattle-barons and wealthy mining men who ruled the wild country.

In the early days of Tombstone he had known Judge Arnold favorably. Now he was glad to be able to repay many acts of kindness by helping his son. Albert Arnold and Harry Smith had been friends for years. Arnold was now only too glad to use his influence in getting him a good position. "San Simon Dick" had proven his worth. His experience and good judgment placing him in a good paying position.

Instead of returning to civilization by the rough

trail down the cañon, they led their horses across
the divide to Ramsey Cañon and then rode along
the lonesome "storm king" trail through Bear
Cañon and down into the dangerous Box Cañon
which breaks the rugged mountain wall bordering on the desert.

Traveling across the desert at that point was
not so very dangerous if one knew the trail. Half
way across the dreary sand waste was a desert
station where the traveler could get plenty of
water and buy provisions at the little store room
kept by a poor health-seeker from the East.

At the sun-baked desert station of "Spanish
tanks" a light is kept burning to show the poor
weary soul who has lost his way in a forlorn endeavor to reach the phantom village and delightful
shady lakes shown him in the mirage, the cause of
many a poor prospector to meet a horrible death
from thirst, that help is near.

At this dreary place a small colony of consumptives live in a forlorn hope that the clear dry air
and even temperature will cure their terrible
malady.

The awful loneliness of the dreary place will
make the inhabitant, if not crazy, decidedly queer.
Here for hours at a time they sit in the straggling
shade of a cottonwood, continually coughing and
barking with that awful rasping graveyard croak
that accompanies the deadly hectic fever. Though
they never lose hope, the poor emaciated frames
are soon laid away on the little knoll just west of
the tanks. All of them come from the North and
East. The doctor and lawyer, farmer and actor,
all go to make up the forlorn colony.

As they approached the station, they could see no signs of life. In the tennis court near the arbor lay a man with his head blown off. Horrified at what they saw, the men dismounted and climbed the fence to examine the body and give the alarm.

Smith recognized the face as one he had seen in Tombstone often. On entering the house, a prairie wolf that had been asleep on top of the table sprang through the window. In the dining-room twelve dead bodies were found, some evidently shot as they were quietly eating supper. Upstairs two more frames were lying in the farther corner of a room, shot full of holes. It was very evident that the purpose of the murderers was not one of robbery, as nothing was disturbed about the premises.

After filling their canteens they hastily mounted and rode away to notify the proper authorities in Bisbee. Only another of those terrible desert tragedies which are altogether of too frequent occurrence. The crazy act of some poor prospector who had lost his reason during one of the long lonesome journeys across the desert, or perhaps some demented member of the household in a fit of insanity had murdered his companions in misery.

The vast solitude of the great Southwest, horrible in its desolation, has a strange influence on the lonely inhabitants of this weird region. A person living on the desert at a ranch, or at one of the lonely desert stations, soon becomes afflicted with that strange disease which is locally known as "fool-in-the-head loco" or plain "bug house."

The first symptoms of the strange affliction are a desire to carry three or four six-shooters tied onto the hip at one time. Hunting a quarrel with some one you know will not fight seems to be another very marked trait of the afflicted. One often hears weird stories as the cowboys, seated around their camp-fires at night, tell of the awful uncanny adventures and strange visitations they have experienced while alone in the darkness and storms of the desert. How all the rivers and watering places of this great Southwestern solitude are haunted and all children born on the desert are left-handed, and should you drink out of a river with your head down stream, you are doomed forever after to be an everlasting liar.

Many cattlemen and prospectors coming into town after long and weary trips over the desert tell uncanny stories of a giant cowboy whom they often meet. Tall and gaunt with large glassy eyes, always wearing a forlorn pleading look on his worn, haggard face, and ever begging for water, he roamed the desert mounted on his fierce wild bronco. Approaching cautiously the long sought drink, his steed, as though terrified, wheels suddenly and disappears in a cloud of sand.

A legend among the old timers has it that a cowboy refused to give a dying prospector a drink of water during the terrible draught of years ago. Dying, the man cursed him and God has willed it that he shall ride forever over the burning sands of the desert, seeking water which this unmanageable steed will not approach. Such are the legens of "The country that God forgot," and on knowing the place one gives them credence.

On leaving the desert station, great haste was
made to reach Bisbee before dark to notify the
coroner and sheriff. As they neared the edge of
the desert, they passed Geronimo's Wells, where
they stopped and watered their animals.

This was another of those colonies occupied by
wealthy consumptives. There were no ghastly
crimes to record here, though most all the occu-
pants were half dead. There was the wealthy
merchant with millions of money and only one
lung. Various grades of doctors and lawyers sat
wearily around listening to a mournful-looking,
dreamy-eyed, one-legged Thespian, serious-vis-
aged and sad, in his most striking endeavor de-
livering one of Shakespeare's .wildest. Heavy
tragedy must have been his forte, for he had his
little audience spellbound except those who, overcome, had fallen asleep.

A crazy sheep-herder rode up on a Mexican
mule and announced himself as the ghost of
Brigham Young. None of this invalid colony
were exactly crazy though they were all decidedly
queer.

As they dismounted to water their horses,
Arnold very cautiously inquired if they had seen
any one pass that way lately who showed any
signs of being loco. The Thespian, who seemed
to be endowed with the most wind power, replied
that a lonely prospector from the mountains of
Mexico had passed that way only two days ago.

He was old and gray, though apparently a man
of great refinement and education. He had with
him some samples of very rich gold rock and
visions of a great bonanza seemed to have turned

his head, for he challenged them one and all to
come out and fight a duel either on foot or
mounted, though he was mounted only on a flop-
eared mangy burro. Very willingly would the
Thespian have fought him a merry bout had he
not been restrained by a sedate lawyer who had
not yet been overcome by the solitude and lost his
reason.

They evidently know nothing of the terrible
tragedy enacted at their neighbor's station just
across the desert and feeling that it would not do
other than cause them great worry and misery in
their already deplorable condition, Arnold did not
inform them, but bidding them a good-bye with a
hearty well wish, he mounted his horse and rode
away, followed by his companions.

They were all men of wealth and evidently of
good social position in their eastern communities.
They seek the desert and its dry cool air, always
hoping against hope and knowing they will only
too soon encounter that inevitable cure, the grave.

As they drew away, the "loco" Thespian burst
in sad verse, written by a health seeker and first
published in the Tombstone Epitaph.

DOOMED
I come to these sands
To enjoy the climate.
Skull and bones,
A frame, animate
Heat and sun
Are my salvation.
I find plenty here
On this desolation

Bale-wire and cans
The deserts decoration.

The wild cowboy howls
His rum-stewed song
While he spurs his
Bucking bronco along.
The burro shrieks out
His mournful wail,
The coyote crones
His sad refrain,
While the buzzard
Wings his lazy way
High up in the sky,
Scanning the sands
With his watchful eye
And patiently waiting
For some one to die.

Wheeling and turning he
Circles about
Slowly drawing nearer
As the life goes out.

Like a wreck on the
Ocean drifting,
Or sand through
The hour glass sifting,
You are doomed,
Poor limb of the devil.
You may do your best
You cannot escape him
Till you're laid at rest.

Arriving in Bisbee they notified the coroner, who left immediately with a jury for the scene of the terrible crime. They could view the remains, give the usual verdict, but search where they might it would still remain another of those terrible unsolved desert mysteries.

The horses were put up in the O. K. corral, a favorite stable for cowboys and miners and the dusty travelers repaired to the "Castle Rock Inn," where very comfortable rooms were obtained at a nominal figure.

"San Simon Dick" lost no time in purchasing the necessary equipment and supplies for his pack train and in four days was on his way again with twenty pack-mules heavily laden with necessities for the mining camp at the mission. Harry Smith accompanied him with a corps of assistants to help survey the claims. Arnold, who had been very busy purchasing supplies and looking after the financial affairs of the company, was now at liberty to look about a little and renew old acquaintances.

He met his friend Warning and was delighted to greet the modest young hero, who was now living in ease, having made a sale of some claims which he owned in Tombstone Cañon. Together they repaired to Old Hankin's store, where they might rest and talk over all times. Hardly had they been seated when to their surprise the tall, manly lookinfg form of Jack Carrol appeared in the doorway, clad in rags and covered with dust and car grease· from head to foot.

A horrible looking "hobo," but one of the best

hearted and truest men who ever rode a Pullman
coach, either on the silk cushions or underneath
on the brake rods. A jolly good handshake all
around and then Carroll excused himself, for as
he said, "You gents will kindly excuse me while
I repair to my apartments and change these rags
for my store clothes. You see, I jest 'breshed' in
on the trimmins of the 'rattler' and ain't had time
to douse myself yet, but still I 'biled out' down at
the stock-yards in Tucson so I ain't so worse.

"No, thanks! got a few plunks left. Yours
truly, but I don't need it. Ain't broke. Just
been making my annual tour before starting on
the fall work. Excuse me, gents, be back in half
an hour."

Arnold and Warning found seats and all the
happenings of the past few months were gone
over. As Arnold was relating in glowing terms
the many adventures of his trip to the San Jose
mountains, Jack Carroll returned, all togged out
in fine style and looking like a cattle baron just
in from the country to "blow" himself.

"Well, here I am and I'm tickled to death to see
you fellows. I've traveled all over the country
since I quit the 'Portage Lake.' Oh, of course it
didn't take me long, you see I never ride anything
but fast specials. Sometimes I had to swing underneath, but generally in fine weather I prefer
to climb up on top where I have better air and a
fine view of the country.

"Yes, I took a fall out of Butte and then paid
my respects to the Rubes in Bucksport, Maine.
That town is the limit. You see I went broke on
a crap game at a Sunday school picnic and for-

getting it was Sunday I hopped into the street to do a song and dance act. Well, you should have seen those 'Rubes' perform. They had the town militia and a hook and ladder company chasing me around for an hour before they landed me in jail.

"The next morning they hauled me into court and as the judge was clearing his throat to say 'Six months,' I bolted and made my get-away. I was nearly starved in Pennsylvania, but done a speel at a camp-meeting and made a few plunks.

"I met an old pal of mine in 'Phille' and together we toured the South. Fine place, New Orleans. Once in a while we got ditched and had to be contented with riding common Pullmans, but that didn't happen very often. Rolled off the 'rattler' at Raleigh; blew up the street, battered a house and got a block of punk.

"Took a fling at Tennessee. We battered a farm house and the old hickory who owned the place just broke down and cried. His wife, an old gray-headed woman, was working in the kitchen and he sings out in a mournful voice, 'Marthie, here's two of them there fellers as what's a going round and round.'

" 'Boys, I'd almost call yeh trampers.'

" 'Take 'em in, Marthie, an' give 'em plenty of that thar corn pone an' hominy.'

" 'Boys,' said the old lady as she placed a great big bowl of cornmeal in front of us, 'did ye ever meet a lad named Willem Sparks, about thirty years old, six foot long, powerful good lookin' an' right pert at figgers?'

"Right there I lost my appetite, for of course I

knew him. Met him four water tanks out of
Denver last summer, so we both excused ourselves
and left.

"We floated down to the depot, been drinking
a little. Bill and I were raising Kane. The law
got wise and throwed his hooks into Bill, but I
dodged and give them the hot foot. They were
gaining on me when just then the rattler came
whizzing by and I made a lam and glued the
trimmin's. The cop caught the hind end and
worked himself along up to where I was, but
having no notion of serving a time in jail, I quit
my perch and climbed into the trucks, forward,
and along to the end, the cop still after me.

"We were going twenty-five miles an hour but
I swung up onto the platform and climbed onto
the roof, the cop hot on my trail. I was soon
chased out of there, but I worked my way ahead
to a cattle car; one of those with the slats about
five inches apart. That cop was bound to get
me. But I had a good start and we flew around
that car like squirrels in a cage. When he was on
one side I was on the other and when I was
on the top he was just turning the under corner.

"Once he caught hold of my coat tail but I made
a switch and pulled loose. We were pulling into
a station. They were going to stop and that cop
would nab me. A fast special carrying a lot of
bankers was just pulling out for New Orleans,
and being about due there, I made a flying leap
and landed on top of her, the 'cop' not daring to
follow. I rode her undisturbed.

"Next morning, being sleepy, I climbed down
and flopped in the grass near a watering tank

after eating a hearty meal of cake, pie, coffee and chicken. The chicken I borrowed from a farmer; the rest of the stuff from the train. I had just about finished my snooze when along comes the roadmaster on a railroad motor car. He stopped and went over to the tank and climbed up to measure the water. Right then I borrowed his machine and flew down to the next town.

"I fired the machine into the ditch and walked down to the end of the yards to catch the first train south. It came by at twenty miles an hour, a fast freight loaded with hobos, thick as fleas on top and underneath. Well, they stopped the train and the 'shack' put us all off. They started on again and of course the wheels hadn't turned twice before we were all seated. They rousted us off, and backed up about a mile to get a good flying start. I swung underneath and as we came whizzing by I reached over to the reserve tanks and released the air, bringing her to a full stop and nearly bouncing her off the rails. Baffled at every turn they let the whole crowd ride, but at the next stop they hauled the whole bunch to jail, but my foot-work was equal to the occasion and I made my 'get-away.'

"That night I rolled into New Orleans and paid my respects to my old pals. Was taken suddenly with chills and fever. I shook so that no one could get by me on the streets. I hired a room in a hotel and being nearly broke, I sat down and wrote a letter to my father, a merchant in Detroit, saying, 'Dear Father, please send me some money, I want to come home. I am broke.' In four days I received a reply, 'My dear son, Jack, may the devil mend you.'

"The old man was wise to his little son alright. I quit that town in a hurry; caught a train for San Antone and made it in style. Was yanked up before the judge when I reached town and locked up for three months. That night I climbed out of the jail without saying good-bye.

"Being somewhat of a hurry I caught a freight train for El Paso, where I met three thousand more 'hobos' from different ends of the country. There was some construction work going on there so I didn't get much dust on me in that village. I caught an armful of gun'nels out of that burg in a hurry.

"As we were dragging along up Stiens-Pass, the 'shack' started to clubbing some of the 'beaus' off. A pretty long train, double header, and not making very fast time, as he was getting pretty near my car, and not caring to get clubbed, I climbed down and pulled the pin. His part of the train went flying down the mountain like a streak.

"We kept right on to the top and down the other side; hopped off at Benson, had four bits in my clothes, went in an' played the wheel, won sixty-five plunks and paid my fare up here. I got a job out at the Marquette shaft any time I care to take it; 'certainly had a grand spin around the country and a jolly good time. I had to work in a rock pile in New Jersey for three days. I hope a cyclone will come along and batter into that town, scattering it all over the earth.

"I had a big feed in Benson down by the stock yards. One 'beau' rustled the 'spuds;' another

bought some onions at his own price ; a third done
the 'elocution' act for some coffee and 'punk,'
while your royal job-lots took a club and knocked
the pins out from under some 'gumps' that were
feeding down near the track.

"I took a spin over to Tucson, met some old
'pals,' camped out down by the creek. We all
had a big feed, 'boiled out' and flopped in the
misquite brush until the International Limited
pulled out for Bisbee when I made a lam and
glued the blind baggage. I climbed into a box-
car on the way up here, and a tougher lot of wild
'beaus' I never met. I got covered with gray-
backs and feel rather suspicious yet.

"I have an invitation to attend a grand
"swauree" to be held at 'Dutch Baker's' place,
'Raw-Hide Manor,' 'Mescal Heights.' I'll have
to shine up some, as some of the heavy swells will
be there. 'Asurite Bill' is going to do the calling
at the dance. Frijoles and beer will be served.
Will you be there?"

"Yes, I'm invited," replied Arnold.

"All right. So long," and with a merry laugh
Carroll departed.

CHAPTER IX.

BISBEE SWELLS.

ALMOST every man in this mining and cattle country came here broke, or badly bent, but by perseverance and dogged determination they have amassed large fortunes in cattle and mines. Some of these hardy men affect the latest styles and dress of the Eastern swell, while others, content in their free and easy life, pay very little attention to their wearing apparel, whether it is the latest style or sixty years behind the times.

Dutch Baker had worked hard in the mines and also found time to take up a few claims and do the required amount of assessment to make the title good. The Copper Queen was the only paying mine in the district at that time. Rich Michigan companies began to buy up the ground and sink shafts. The man who had been laughed at a few years ago was now a wealthy man, having sold his claims for a cool half million.

Dutch Baker had worked hard and lived on beans and sour dough biscuits in his little one-roomed cabin, shingled all over with tin cans and boiler plate, built up on the hill known as "Mescal Heights" near the Pittsburg shaft. In his days of prosperity he could well afford to build the grand mansion by the side of his first humble cabin.

"Rawhide Manor" he named it, and here he was wont to hold a grand "swauree" and jublication, as he called his socials. These parties were not what might be called invitation affairs, for everyone was welcome as long as he conducted himself properly. You could wear a plug hat or go barefoot; wear broadcloth or come in rags; evening suit or digging clothes. It was all the same as long as you acted the gentleman.

The "Elite" of "Quality Hill" generally departed as the "Chloride Chorus" broke in with that sweet refrain entitled "Hard Rock Miners." Many grizzled old timers were in attendance; men who had fought Indians and Mexicans here in the early days of the camp. They looked upon any function in town as incomplete without their attendance. They were only too glad to shake a few measures with the pretty belle of Bisbee, and their heavy measured tread as they balanced and swung with the light-footed beauties showed that they were young in heart, though their feet were decidedly heavy.

The opening song was a duet by "Chloride Bill" and "Gumy-sack Riley," entitled "Mines and Millions," by Scott. This was generally received with great applause. The Brewery Gulch Band whaled out a few tunes. Then Dutch Baker brought down the house with his inimitable style and delivery as he rendered his well-known original poem entitled, "The Desert Steamboat."

Oh! My Burro is my boat
And o'er the sands I float,
With a rusty gun and a
Mangy dog.
Crummy blankets and a
Slab of "hog."
My burro so lazy,
Myself half crazy,
I stake him out at the
Fall of night
And flop on the desert
Till broad daylight.

I've been sober now for
One long hour.
There'll be a good "swauree"
When I end this tour.
If I strike it rich
I'll take every bum
An' croak him dead
With a barrel of rum.

This long-eared devil
Has a terrible wail,
An' o'er the sands
Where e'er I sail
You can hear his
Lonesome Haw! E! Haw!
Wheel!—Awe!—Wheel!—
Whee! ee!—Haw! E! Haw!
Haw! E! Haw!—Aw!—a!

I prod an' club an'
Cuss him flat.

Cuss him in Dutch an'
Spanish four hands roun'
Swing you' pardners
An' cuss him again,
It's club an' cuss
An' cuss an' club
From early in th' mo'nin
Till past sundown
But you can't change the
Notions of this long-ear clown,

He'll mope along th' desert
Like a broken down snail
Lay the wood to his ribs
An' keep a twistin' his tail
Keep a-proddin' an' a-cussin'
An' a clubbin' an' a-fightin',
But you watch out or
He'll shed that pack.
It's all th' same, be it
Jennie or Jack
An' you can't catch 'em
With a streak of lightnin'.

This recitation brought forth great applause,
and so well and favorably was it received that he
had to recite it twice. Gus Hickory, who killed
four Apache Indians by running them to death
out in the San Simon valley, did a monologue
act, and acquitted himself favorably.

Arnold was asked to sing, but modestly declined, though his soft southern voice was away
ahead of any here. He well knew that it was
range, not quality, that was wanted at these gath-

erings. Jack Carroll, fresh from many adventures back in the States, recited a few of his adventures which he had set to rhyme.

"The weather's getting hot
And I've got a big roll,
So I'll quit my job
And take a little stroll.
I glued the trimmin's
On the rattler,
Then climbed on top,
Fine place to view the
Country and a
Dandy place to flop.

Eighty miles right down
To Benson, 'fore
We ever made a stop,
As we dragged into the depot,
I kept an eye out for the cop
As he rubbered up the line
For a chance to soak a fine,
But he'll be "gapping"
There forever, for
I'd already ducked to cover.

Walked up the track
A little higher,
Made a lam and
Caught the next one,
Nailed the good old
Sunset flyer.
As I jumped and
Caught the "blind"

Just ten more
Swung on behind.

As she coughed and
Smoked her funnel
Seven more swung
On the gun'ale.
Happy, reckless, daring pack,
A few too many
For the "shack."
So we rode her undisturbed
To the city of the Angels,

Took a ride to San "Berdu."
Some one rolled me
For my money.   I
Had not a markee—sou,
Took a look at good old "Sack."
Here I'm lucky—met a shack.
Mined with him in Mexico,
Occupied the first two bunks,
So he dumped me fifteen plunks.
This I kept till Oregon
Once more found me
On the bum.

Climbed aboard the first
Fast special that would
Take me to St. Paul,
There was lots of business doing,
Plenty work there in the fall,
But I've always been unlucky,
I am sure a holy fright.
I'm too weak for work that's heavy,

And too strong for work that's light.
Then I roam the wild world over,
From the mountains to the sea,
And any old place I flop at night
Means dreams—sweet dreams—to me.

So I go and grab the "puffer,"
One that's loaded down with grain
Ride that rattler to the limit,
Right into the State of Maine.
Among these "Rubes" I raised
The devil.
This is strong, but on
The level, they were armed
With scythe and dagger,
With their longest hook and ladder,
Men and women in a row,
Armed for fight with axe and hoe,
Came a streaming on my trail,
Howling out a mournful wail,
But I had no thought of fail
And of spending months in jail,
Or of death from that wild pack,
So I lit out for the track.

As the train came whizzing by,
I easily caught her on the "fly,"
And to those "Rubes" it all must seem
That they were only in a dream.
They did not know
As they rubbed their lamps,
That I was Prince of Hobos,
And King of Tramps.
I'd been chased pretty hard,

So up on top
I stretched myself out
For a nice quiet flop.

Rode her into Tennessee,
Had one grand big jamboree.
Took a fling at New Orleans,
That big city on the river,
Here I had the shakes and fever.
Hiked along to San Antone,
Rode the head-end all alone.
Quit that village in a hurry.
I never cause the cops to worry,
For they surely had their woes,
Trying to manage all the "beaus."

Then I lammed and caught the trimmings,
Rode her right on into Benson,
Made a switch and lammed another,
Climbed on top, and there laid down.
My appearance may belie me,
But I rode her into town.
Hadn't been here twenty minutes
Till I got an invitation
To this dance and jublication."

And with a grand and most impressive bow,
Carroll took his seat amidst the greatest hilarity
and uproarious applause.

A happy-go-lucky, good-natured fellow, well
able to sing a song or do the latest stunt in clogs
and dances, he was always welcome at these
"Germans."

A good hand at spinning a yarn, if you felt a

little homesick and wanted to exchange a few
words with somebody about your home town, he
was the man to pitch into, for though he might
not know the names of every man in town, he
certainly could give you an exact description of
the landscape about the depot and picture the
scenes about the water tank faithfully enough to
bring tears to the eyes of the toughest old
"dynamiter."

Just at this point of the entertainment, "Dog-
face Dick" tried to ride his mustang into the reception room. Such a terrible breach of etiquette
was frowned on by every one at the party, and
the unruly guest quietly informed that the affair
would be a howling success without his presence.

"Mustang Mike" nearly broke up the party
when he recited that stirring, original cowboy
ballad, composed by "San Simon Dick" and recited by him with great effect at the Cattlemen's
Convention in Tucson. I can recollect only a
few of the original seventy-nine verses.

"THE WILD COWBOY."

There was a wild cowboy,
Called San Simon Dick,
With a ten-bore six-shooter
He was sure lightnin' quick.
From his ranch on the range,
Now just for a change,
He mounted and rode into town,
His throat full of dust,
His clothes all in rags,
On his face a horrible frown.

He rode to the door
Of the Chemical Works
And called for some wood alcohol.
They gave him enough
To produce a wild fit,
And in wild howling glee,
He rode in to see what
The inside of a gin mill was like.

Now the marshal inside with a
Long measured stride
And a rifle tucked under
Each arm paced the room
That was silent as the house of the dead.
At the first sign of danger
He turned his head
And filled that wild cowboy
Chucked full of cold lead.
Then turning in terror,
He bolted and fled with a howl
That was heard near and far,
For that cowboy was rolling
A brown cigarette.
And his horse smoked
A long green cigar.

With his rapid-fire gun
He smashed all the glass,
While his horse drove his
Hoofs through the bar.
Then he threw a half-hitch
'Round his chest with his arms,
And coughed up that lead on the floor.
Let me tell you right here,

'Fore I move from my tracks,
These here are simply the statement of facts.

There was twenty-six pounds
Of lead in that pile,
And while on his face
He wore a broad smile,
He mounted his mustang
And plunged through the door
With a wild ringing yell
Like the devil in hell,
He flew down the gulch,
On destruction he surely was bent.
With a gun in each hand,
He stormed through the town
And shot out the lights
As he went.

The yell that greeted this recitation nearly
lifted the roof off the mansion, and right then and
there the literary editor of the "Tombstone Epitaph" leaped to his feet and in a few well-chosen
words said a meeting should be called to form a
literary society, which he proposed should be
called "The Cañon Club," and composed only of
members who lived in Dixie Cañon, Tombstone
Cañon or Brewery Gulch, Quality Hill and School
Hill. A committee was chosen to call a meeting,
and then "Dutch" Baker announced a recess so
that the men could go out and have a few drinks
and smoke, while the women chewed gum and
exchanged town gossip.

When the intermission was over, "Dutch"
Baker mounted the platform and delivered one

of those timely speeches which had made him
famous in camp. In a loud, stentorious voice he
delivered his best oration.

After rolling up his pants legs and unbuttoning
his heavy blue flannel shirt, to give him more free-
dom of limb and neck, he strode across the floor
to a stand in the corner, and deliberately helped
himself to a glass of water.

Three men fainted dead away when they saw
that, but the meeting went merrily on. He threw
out his chest, spat on his hands, and emphasizing
his remarks with a heavy fist, lit right in.

"Ladies an' Fellow Gentlemen! As I stand
before you, I feel it my duty to thank all of you
for the appreciation you all have shown towards
me in honoring my mansion with your presence.
I owe my success to my close attention to business and clear understanding of human nature.
I've been in close scrapes many times. Once out
on the desert the Apaches jumped my trail. We
had a smooth stretch of country, but a fleet-footed
wildcat obstructed my path. Just to show them
Injuns I was no slouch I spoke right up an' says—
remember I was still at high speed—I says in a
rage: 'Get out uv th' road, you damn lumberin'
fools an' let a man run as knows how.' "

"You can bet y'ur pile agin' th' whole bank roll
that I left them Injuns meditatin' on th' sands.

"Of course, I'm th' oldest prospector on th'
desert, every one in these yer diggin's knows
that. When I was in Mexico last summer, down
on the gold coast, I was took sick, and to add to
my troubles, I was arrested by the Mexican authorities as a political suspect. Of course, I felt

flattered just a little, but that feelin' soon wore
off.

"You see how my shoulders are broken and
twisted. Well, those greasers were told by their
commander to disarm me. They didn't understand English very well, but flew at me with a
will. Took away my revolver and rifle, and then
began pulling and hauling at my arms. I tried to
talk them out of it, but 'twas no use.

"Arms are dangerous weapons, and there were
my shoulder blades, more dangerous still. I
might cut someone's head off with them. I
started to run with three men on my back, the
soldiers began firing, but I was so completely
covered with Mexicans, I escaped unharmed.

"We're all peaceable citizens, ain't we? Some
folks will tell you that cowboys eat Gila monsters and sage-brush. Well, they do, sometimes,
if served up with whiskey, but as a rule they are
gentle an' tame. But for them fellows the Mexicans would have recaptured me. But by their
aid I travelled all night, and crossed the line near
the old custom-house. That's a fine piece of
architecture, built on the perpendicular side of a
semi-circular square. The officer in charge was
a fine gentleman and very learned.

"We talked for a few hours—him throwin' out
some heavy Greek names pretty often, but I
stayed with him, and just to show him I was no
slouch as a scholar, I'd recite a little heavy litera-
ture, once in a while giving him some Chinee and
Indian talk, mixed with signs and a little lingo
like that. Well, I guess it took him by surprise
all right.

"I've been shot so many times, and my carcas is so full of lead, that when I get overheated, the molten metal just runs out through the pores of my hide. I'm the oldest prospector in these yah diggin's, an' a tough one, too. I'm tougher en hell. I ask yah pardon, feller ladies an' gents, but that slipped out 'fore I could shut the gate, but I'm sure a powerful old-timer an' they can't kill me.

"I cum near dying of over-exertion last summer when I overdid myself breakin' in a clean pair of socks, but I managed to stay on the earth. Then I had the fever. I came awful near being planted, but I pulled through. I was so thin I could step into a double-barrel shotgun, an' have a swell pair of pants. A rattlesnake bit me an' died. You know there is a popular saying that all animals are afraid of man except the 'grayback.' Well, a bunch of wildcats jumped me one day out on Copper Cross Mountain, an' I whipped the whole bunch in two seconds. Well, I've speeched long enough. My throat's gettin' dry. D'ye think I'm a camel—never drink? I made this yah speech just to show you I am well edge-kated, an' have good command of my mouth an' the English language—the result of deep research, observation, culture an' travel.

"We will now close this heah meetin' by singing that well-known little ballad entitled 'Looking through the Knot-hole in Grandpa's Wooden Leg.'"

Evidently greatly pleased with himself as an entertainer, old "Dutch" Baker threw out his arms with heavy measured swings and beat time with the same motion and energy he would use with a shovel or pick-axe.

They were just starting in on the last verse with a vim that sent electric shocks through the whole audience, when suddenly the door opened and hump-backed Clancy, an old gray-headed prospector with a wild determined look in his eye, strolled in and walked across the room in front of the genial host without noticing him. He strolled leisurely across the floor, with his hat dangling in his hands, which were folded peacefully behind his back.

Now, every man has his suspicious beliefs, and old Dutch was no exception. He made it a rule to always rub backs with a hump-backed man, and always give chase to a black cat.

For the morning he struck pay dirt on his mining claim, thereby becoming a millionaire, he rubbed backs with old hump-backed Clancy, and to make the sign more binding he chased a black cat off his cabin. If he let the chance slip by, it surely would bring bad luck, and being somewhat acquainted with the old man he did not think it would cause more than a little laughter among the audience. But since it had been noised about camp how old "Dutch" Baker won his fortune on the luck that "Hump-back" Clancy brought him, it got to be a regular practice for every miner or cowboy who wanted a little good luck to blow his way, to catch old Clancy whenever they could find him, and rub backs. Now, this good-hearted old prospector shared this belief, but of late he had lost some of his fortune, and as old "Dutch" leaped from the platform to the floor with his heavy miner's shoes, landing with the noise of an earthquake, "Hump-back" Clancy took fright and shot across the room like a frightened wildcat, turned the corner and flew down the side aisle with old "Dutch" in close pursuit. The audience, taken by surprise with this sudden change of programme, stood aghast; but soon divining the purpose of old Baker's strange actions, they quickly fell in behind, each one feeling that whoever caught the coveted prize would win a fortune.

Around the room they fairly flew, old Clancy straining every muscle to escape his fleet-footed pursuers. The old prospector was holding his own, but on the tenth round old "Dutch" Baker leaped forward in sheer desperation and grabbed him by the leg. Both men plunged heavily into the corner, where twenty more eager pursuers filed up on top of them.

When the howling, squirming pile was finally separated and the dead and mangled counted, it was found that four dead and fifteen injured was the result of the stampede.

Both "Dutch" Baker and old Clancy escaped alive, and of course had one more hair-breadth escape to relate when they met at the Miners' Congress in old Dan Hankins' store.

When the result of the accident was noised about town, there were expressions of sorrow heard on all sides. For among the dead were "Dish-rag" George and "Coal-oil" Jimmie, two of the best-known miners in the district.

They had been partners for years, and only the week before had struck it rich on their claim out at the "White-tail Deer." For years they had

worked and struggled—sometimes pay dirt—
sometimes in debt, but they never lost heart, and
at last struck it rich.

A true fissure vein which assayed seven thousand dollars to the ton brought them in a comfortable fortune, and great was the sorrow when
the facts of their deaths became known.

The coroner's jury, after viewing the bodies
and visiting the scene of the accident, rendered
the following verdict: "We the jury, find that
the victims met death at the hands and feet of a
mob in 'Rawhide Manor,' and solemnly recom-
mend their souls to God.

Signed: "Pete Johnson, Foreman."

Great preparations for the funerals were made,
and the next day the solemn cortege slowly
wound its way around the bend in Brewery
Gulch, and down Tombstone Cañon to the graveyard on the hillside just back of the junction mining shaft.

As the funeral procession moved slowly out of
town an awful silence settled over the whole
camp.   Old "Dutch" Baker and "Hump-back"
Clancy, dressed in deep mourning and seated on
an ore wagon, led the procession.

The next in line was the Bisbee Fire Department in red shirts and helmets.   They marched
with a solemn stride, and in vain tried to keep
step with the dirge played by the Chloride Band.

The dead prospectors had been well and favorably known in Tombstone in the early days, and
that city honored their memory by sending over
the gallant old Cloudburst Fire Company.

They made a fine appearance as they marched hay-foot, straw-foot down the cañon.

Bringing up the rear of the procession was a motley array of cowboys, miners, prospectors, Mexicans and Indians. Even the old Chinaman gardener from Fairbanks came to pay his respects to the dead, walking side by side with "Bronco Sal," who had on more than one occasion been the object of the dead miner's liberality at her home up on Brewery Gulch, known as the smooth-bore hog ranch. Poor old "Dish-rag" George, kind-hearted to a fault, he would take a handful of silver in one hand, and a handful of rocks in the other, and let fly, either one with the greatest liberality and unconcern. Maybe he couldn't fight—just walk up, kick him in the ribs and see him rear up and snort. Gamble—why he would bet his last dollar on the number of snores he let out during the night. Play faro—copper the Jack and play the ace high, or pile up his bets and play a last chance on the cut.

Well, all processions must have an end, and this one was no exception. After the last sad rites were over, the mourners returned to town, and the broken-hearted miners and cowboys drowned their sorrows in a grand horse race and shooting contest.

For both "Dish-rag" George and "Coal-oil" Jimmie were worthy of a grand send-off, and their friends meant to give them a fare-thee-well that would be remembered in the camp for years to come.

The night was spent in wild drinking and reckless orgies, but the next day the camp shook off

its funeral colors and everything swung along in
the same old style.

In the mad reveille I only caught a few lines of
the song sung by the Cowboys' Quartette.

Here they are:

"Roll your tail an' roll it high,
We'll be with the Angels by an' by,
Then bury me out on the lone prairie,
Where the wild coyotes howl o'er my grave."

To a stranger just in from the States, the desert
stations and lonely mining camps in the wild
mountainous country, so rough that a crow flying
over would tear its shadow to pieces, are interesting places to visit.

One may hear tales of rich mining claims on
every hand, for no miner or prospector ever
owned a claim that did not assay away up in the
thousands, to hear him tell it, though he may be
afraid to take a sample from the indications, for
fear the ore would pinch out.

Any old prospector is ever ready to defend his
assertions that his mining claim is the richest in
the world, though it may assay pretty heavy in
pyrites of poverty and carry good indications of
continual starvation.

The wandering miner who in fits of fancy flit-
ters here and there is always ready with some
fault-finding argument about the last camp he
worked in, and though he may be so thin you
could tie a knot in the seat of his breeches, he is
sure to unload that yarn of how he whipped the
shift-boss and called down the whole works.

He won't forget to criticize his fellow work-men about their honesty and neatness, though he has a tendency to let his hand take a cramp on anything worth swiping, and his ready-made suit of rags are very apt to be covered with seam squirrels and rapid-transit bugs.

He will curse the camp and damn the judge who fined him for the heinous offence of being drunk and disorderly and refusing to fight.

He will roar at the grub and blow about his cooking ability and pitch a fit if he hears you call anything on the table a mulligan stew, and lose no time in telling you that, though you may cook a meal in tin cans down in the jungles, it is no mulligan unless it's cooked with railroad ties.

You may hammer out a stew, but it's no mulligan without the ties.

He has worked with tarriers, chaws, dog-eaters, bear-dancers, cousin jacks, single jacks, double jacks, jack Mormons and jack asses, and he is never bashful about telling you that he is a better miner than anything in the whole bunch.

He will put you wise to the fact that a machine man ties a string of washers around his neck and puts a small monkey-wrench in his pocket so that all may know what kind of a miner he is.

He will explain how the man who handles the single jack ties a piece of fuse around his waist and a mucker ties a piece of rope around his legs, just about the calves, to denote the different grade they belong to, but a "mule" must be guessed at, for there is no way to tell just what branch of the service he is in until you hear him bray.

Here are a few of his rules for the mine boss:

To make a good "mule"—Take a tame cowboy and knock his brains out with a pick handle. Then tie him up to the ore chute for a few days and comb him gently with a club. Then throw him down the shaft a few times to toughen him, and he is ready for work.

To make your digging rags last—Don't leave anything in the change-room but your old fuse and your wire candlestick.

He deeply deplores the use of slang among the miners and prides himself on his beautiful diction. Here is a sample of his battered language in his story of the wreck on the main line:

"I understand," began the superintendent of the division to the hobo miner whom he had called up on the carpet to explain about the wreck, "I understand that you were traveling through the country riding with my train-crew: a tourist as it were."

"Now, baldy, yer lammed her square in the centre," replied the miner. "I was scootin' across the scenery flyin' light as a July rabbit. Yer train got ditched an' here's how she happened:

"The hoghead was down greasing the hog; the tallowpot was up crackin' the black dimonds; the breakie was over rumblin' the bums; the hobos were glommin' the trimmins; the hine shack was out bendin' the steel; Casey asleep at the switch, there was nobody there with the rag, she flopped over on her back in the ditch an' that's how she got it.

"I'll roll me a pill, baldy, an' I'm on me way."

He never overlooks a chance to rawhide a man

just learning to run a machine through when he
first hired out as a machine man and the boss sent
him and his partner to work in the stope and told
them they would find a machine in the drift at the
foot of the manway, which they were to haul into
the stope, set up and drill a round of holes.

The shift-boss came around in due time, expecting to find holes enough drilled to blow up
the whole mine, but to his surprise he found the
two rubes with a big rope tied securely around
the hand-pump, which they were very carefully
hoisting up into the stope, when Mr. Boss let a
yell that sent them flying down the drift and
caused them to go walking down the cañon talking to themselves.

That kind of a miner is met with in almost any
old mining camp from Butte to Bisbee, and of
course he always knows it all.

He is continually on the wing, and here is a
poem illustrative of his flighty character, written
by the "off-wheeler" and recited by him at the
funeral of "Death Valley Slim:"

"A HARD ROCK MINER."

"Are you the mug
What hires a plug
To work in this yere mine?"
Inquired the woolly dynamiter
Just in from the main line.
"I am the foreman
Of all these works;
I keep the good hands
And fire the shirks.

Are you a miner ?"
"Dam sight better one
Than you are;
I've worked everywhere."
"I need a few men
To give me a lift.
Come out in the morning,
I'll try you a shift."
Next morning the boss
Surveyed him all round
And told him just where
To work underground.
In deep meditation and
Concealing his rage,
He grabbed up his grub can
And climbed on the cage,
Then slowly descended
The rickety shaft
And made ready right there
To begin the day's graft.
With the steel on his back,
He flew up the track,
Struck the heat
And slowed down to a mope.
Then shifting his load
And fixing his light,
He slowly climbed
Into the stope
Though he dropped
Half the steel
On his partner.
He scattered holes
In the breast
Without taking a rest,

Chewed the rag
About cramps
Which on different tramps
Had proved not quite
To his liking,
And caused him
To take to the trails
Once again
And continue his
Cross-country hiking.
When he' worked
The eight shift
He rolled down the drift
And stopped on the station
To explain his relation
With all dam'd outfits
Who handled the dough,
Remarking that money
Thus made with the hammer
Was certainly coming
A little too slow
Then he rode to the top
Without making a stop,
Ran to the depot
And climbed under the train.
He seated himself
Up on the trucks
And counted his dough.
He had just thirteen bucks,
So he glued to the gunnels
And flew o'er the track
Till hauled from his roost
By the burly old shack.

He had ditched all his rags,
So with fifteen more vags
They dodged 'round the depot
To escape the town bull,
And hiked up the hill
Where the train had to pull
So slow it was surely
Dead easy to make.
They were now flying light
As a gray July rabbit,
So she flew down the grade
And each station they made
So fast that the tracks
All seemed lined with
Depots, freight houses and shacks.
They rolled on and on,
They sure had the moving notion,
And I guess that you'll find
They are traveling yet,
For they are men of
Perpetual motion.

The tenderfoot from the East will not find it
necessary to lose an eye in trying to discover a
slight difference in the drama as played on Broadway and at the lonely desert stations in the great
white sand.

Here is an authentic account of the only grand
opera ever pulled off at the Lone Wolf trading
post, where the heavy villain escaped without being pumped full of lead:

Three knocks on the floor with a club was the
signal for the Indian squaw to hoist away on the

life line and pull the rawhide curtain up to the
ceiling.

In the first spasm Romeo gave Juliet a poke in
the slats that pretty near queered the girl, but
Jule was good on the comeback and soused his
nibs on the snoot with a wicked mit that nearly
put the bloke into dreamland.

After a short intermission and free-for-all fight
Don Coyote in four bouts, with Death Valley Slim
as the leading man, was played and proved a
howling calamity, for the Don, who was supposed
to have the sign of the bug in his head, tried to
act like a loco sheepherder, and a wild cowboy,
just in from the bush, put him off the open range
into poor pasture with a rap on the jaw.

CHAPTER X.

A RANGER.

MINING had taken a jump in the great Bonanza circle and shafts were being sunk in all directions. Everything was booming and owing to the feverish excitement and influx of all kinds of desperate characters, lawlessness and robbery were the orders of the day.

The officers of the ranger force were unable to cope with the situation, owing to lack of numbers, and Capt. Ryan, in looking around for good material, offered Albert Arnold a commission, knowing that he was absolutely trustworthy, brave and cool under trying circumstances.

Arnold would have refused but at the earnest solicitation of his employer, who was already beginning to feel the sting of the outlaw bands, he decided to accept the position and was accordingly sworn in as a member of the force.

Being sober and industrious, thoroughly understanding the nature of his duties and knowing the desert and mountains like a book, he felt it would not take long to rid the country of such cutthroats as were able to dodge around the mountains, relying on their knowledge of the country to elude the officers who were constantly on their trail.

Being stationed in the mining district, and as almost all of his work would be along the Mexican line, he could attend to his duties with the mining company and help rid the country of its tough characters at the same time.

Though he had been in a few crooked transactions himself, Arnold felt that he was justified in what he had done to regain his property. He had always been straightforward and square, and felt that he had only stolen back that which the Mormons had stolen from him. Or, as he explained it to some friends, in his quaint Southwestern intonation, he had only negotiated a forced loan.

Chacon, the brutal murderer from Clifton, had broken jail and was now terrorizing the ranches and mining camps along the Border.

Colonel Kosterlisca with his Mexican Rurales had either hung or driven out all the cutthroats in the State of Sonora. Some of them had crossed the line and disappeared in the onward rush. Others, and the majority, were still at their old tricks of robbing stages, holding up trains and here and there making a raid on some lonely ranch.

As Arnold was true and possessed a very level head, Captain Ryan of the Rangers assigned him to the capture of Chacon, the brutal Mexican outlaw.

He had held up the town of Metcalf, near Clifton, and killed a score of people in making his escape.

At night he would sneak up to some ranch

house and shoot the unsuspecting settler through the back.

Members of hunting and camping parties out in the mountains had been found shot to death, and shot from behind, as they sat around their campfire at night.

To rid the territory of this monster was a dangerous undertaking, but nevertheless it must be done, and Captain Ryan assigned young Arnold to the much dreaded task. His knowledge of the country and language would help him, but he was hunting a man whose cunning had kept him free for years, when the country fairly swarmed with officers. Many men had taken up the task, disguised themselves as Mexicans and gained an entrance into his circle of intimate and trusty cutthroat friends, only to be found out and slain.

Arnold confided his secrets to his staunch friends, "San Simon Dick" and Harry Smith, who were very busy, each at the head of his own department, surveying and transporting supplies to the mining camp. To his great surprise he also learned that the camp up in the San Jose mountains had been honored or dishonored by a visit from the much wanted Chacon.

He had appeared at their camp unannounced, and after stating that he was a poor prospector and in need of some supplies, which were given him, he departed as mysteriously as he had come. This visit spread great consternation in camp as the pack trains were carrying out large quantities of gold ore on each trip, it was feared that "San Simon Dick" would be attacked, robbed and killed by the outlaw and his bloody cutthroats.

"San Simon Dick" was in a rage and swore he would fight the whole outfit single handed. But he was not likely to meet them at all, that was unnecessary in the wild, rocky and majestic Hauchucas were deep cañons and towering peaks afforded the finest chance in the world to shoot the lonely traveler as he slowly picked his way along the narrow dangerous trail.

Arnold saw his only chance, so he returned to the mining camp with the pack train and laid bare his plans. On arriving in camp he had a long talk with Captain Ryan of the Rangers.

His plan of campaign was to return to the mountains with "San Simon Dick," who knew every trail and watering place like a book, and watch the springs, for he very well knew that any man leaving the country would have to come out through the great wild, rugged cañon and stop for water at the Troopers' Rest Springs. Or if the other trail were taken, the traveler would have to pick his way along the narrow shelf of rock overhanging Montezuma Cañon, where a misstep meant death among the rocks a thousand feet below.

The narrow ledge along Bright Angels' Trail had been condemned and blown up by the army officers from Fort Huachuca, as it was too dangerous to travel.

The person coming out through the very dangerous Montezuma Cañon would have to get water at Soldiers' Gardens. Of course, Dripping Springs Ranch was just as near, but outlaws had a wholesome respect for Colonel Bill Cornell or anything that bore his brand.

He always let everyone alone and he was the
first man in the country that everyone was very
careful to let entirely alone. It was decided
that Arnold should watch the springs at Soldiers'
Gardens and "San Simon Dick" was entrusted
with the task of guarding "Troopers' Rest"
Springs. The outlaw was just as liable to travel
one trail as the other. He might leave the mountains in a day, or he might not leave for six
months.

"Nigger Ned" and "Malachite Mike" had quit
work and were busy keeping a bright lookout
over their property.

"Malachit- Mike" had been fired on one day
as he was treating some gold ore at the arrastra
which had been used years ago by the Spaniards.

Affairs were getting pretty serious. People
in Bisbee and Tombstone said it would be the
same old, old story: "Two lonely prospectors
found murdered in their cabin away up in the
lonely, wild, haunted mountains." It would be
passed along as another of those awful unex-
plained tragedies of the great solitude.

All work at the claims was stopped. Every
precaution was taken to prevent an ambush. The
springs were closely guarded. Weeks passed
and no outlaw made his appearance.

A Ranger brought word that all the invalids
at the health resort up in the mountains back of
the fort had been held up and robbed. They
were so excited they could give no definite description of the road agent who had made the
forced loan.

Arnold had grown tired of his solitary vigil,

and sent word by a carrier for "San Simon
Dick" to meet him at Colonel Cornell's ranch.

Chacon, the Mexican murderer, must have
made his way to Mexico for no trace of him was
to be had in Arizona.

Colonel Kosterlisca and his Rurales were
patrolling the border. A terror to evil doers, he
had a way of filling the outlaw murderers full of
lead, and then giving them the formality of a trial
afterwards.

Chacon, desperado and professional cutthroat,
was far too wise to try to break through his
battalion of crack guardsmen. "San Simon
Dick" arrived at the Dripping Springs Ranch,
and there met Colonel Cornell, who had just returned from his copper mines in La Cananea,
Mexico.

Arnold rode up to the ranch late that night and
in the moonlight, quietly seated on the veranda,
the three men held a council of war.

Colonel Cornell was decidedly "riled up," as
old Murphy would say. "Everything must go
ahead and go ahead with a jump. Dead greaser
or dead gringo, I am going to open up that mine
and now that the indications are so favorable we
start in immediately to taking out pay dirt.

"This cutthroat business must stop. I have
offered a substantial reward and I will keep raising it until one of those cutthroat outlaws are
worth as much as a gold mine.

"This bluff game is about played out. Three
fellows tried it over in Naco last week and met
their deaths from an overdose of cold lead." It
was very evident the Colonel meant business.

Arnold was advised to return to Bisbee and look after supplies.

"San Simon Dick" was to return to his pack trains and rush supplies into the camp; hire guards if he wished to but the necessities for working the mines must be rushed in without delay.

After laying plans for the morrow they all retired. Arnold climbed to the top of the flat roofed adobe ranch house, and there stretched himself out on a canvas cot for a nice quiet sleep. "San Simon Dick" must have received some kind of a hunch that trouble was brewing, for he refused the honor of sleeping in the ranch house, and after turning his saddle horse into the corral, with a bunch of high blooded stock which had just arrived from the Colonel's ranch in Arizona, he climbed the hay-stack at the corner of the coral and there stretched himself out for a good rest.

Intermittently the horrible croaks of the deep braying burro could be heard as he gave answer for answer from one end of the desert to the other. The coyotes and wolves, mountain lions and wild cats vied with one another from their lone mountain peaks or dreary sand drifts to see who would be the first to wake the dead.

Their howls and half human shrieking is music to the lonely cowboy as he lays wrapped in his blankets on some soft sand pile out on the desert or stretched full length peacefully sleeping on a high shelf of rock away up in the wild rugged mountain peaks of the southwestern Rockies, or lost in sweet slumber on a shifting sand bar down in the dark, dismal depths of the dreary danger-

ous cañons, sublime in their loneliness, awful and
grand in their silence and solitude. But let the
rythm of their song be broken, let a twig snap
and he is wide awake and on his feet in a second
with his ready gun within reach, that he may
swing it into action in a second if danger should
beset him.

"San Simon Dick" was no exception to the
rule. During the intermittent howling of the
wolves a silence seemed to prevail over the whole
place and instinctively he awoke and raising himself on his elbow, listened. He could plainly hear
footsteps walking on the dry sun-flower stalks
in the corner of the corral. He eased himself
over to the edge of the stack on his hands and
knees and peered cautiously down into the corral,
though careful not to expose his head to view,
keeping it well back under the horizon line, he
could see all that was happening below.

There in the corral stood a man, lasso in hand,
trying to catch his saddle horse, the best one in
the corral, or in the country for that matter.

In deep meditation he watched the proceedings.
Was it a horse thief, or some cowboy saddling
up to go out on guard with the night herd? If it
was, who gave him permission to take his horse?

Evidently the horse had his own notions about
night work for he seemed to have no intention of
being caught. The stranger stood in the shadow
of the smoke house, but presently in trying to
corner the horse he stepped out into the full glow
of the southwestern moonlight, and to the utter
amazement of "San Simon Dick" he beheld the

gigantic form of the Mexican murderer and outlaw—Chacon.

There could be no mistake—the tall form,, the
crippled leg, great broad shoulders and deep
heavy chest. There he stood—murderer a dozen
times, with a lasso in one hand and a big heavy
six-shooter in the other.

Will a horse know a murderer? Yes, a horse
raised on the wild free range will detect his presence among a thousand men.

So eagerly was the murderer endeavoring to
catch a mount that he did not perceive he was
being watched. Very slowly and cautiously
"San Simon Dick" raised a slight screen of hay
in front of himself and peered through, for
though the outlaw was now walking with is back
to him, there was great danger of exposing his
head above the horizon line and thereby causing
the animals in the corral to throw up their heads
and survey his position, causing the outlaw to
take to cover, or still there might be some one on
watch ready to shoot the first man who put in
an appearance.

Evidently the outlaw had great patience and
was wholly ignorant of the fact that he was
closely watched.

"San Simon Dick" worked his rifle into range
and then watched every movement of the outlaw.
He could easily fill him full of lead, but shooting
a man in the back from ambush was something he
was not capable of doing.

Finally the outlaw succeeded in lassoing the
very elusive saddle horse, and now perfectly gentle and submissive with a lasso around his neck

he permitted himself to be tied to a post and saddled.

As the deep heavy riding saddle settled noiselessly into place "San Simon" indulged in a quiet little laugh, which seemed to shake the whole hay-stack. He knew very well that any man who tried to ride his horse would either have to kill the horse or kill himself in the attempt. He always boasted that his horse could throw the best rider on the range without taking a hoof off the ground.

The outlaw took great pains in cinching up the saddle and evidently figured on covering a long stretch of desert before daylight.

After closely inspecting the saddle and bridle, Chacon led his borrowed mount out through the corral gate and after securely fastening it again, he placed a high power carabine in the saddle scabbard and very gracefully swung himself into the saddle and just as gracefully was sent skyward by the powerful loose-limbed bronco who knew but one master. That was just what "San Simon Dick" had been expecting, and grasping his rifle, he slid down the hay-stack and ran to the unconscious form lying spread-eagle near the saddle horse.

He quickly tied him hand and foot and as he straightened up to draw his six-shooter and fire a few shots to arouse the ranch, a hail of bullets whizzed over his head, coming from a break of sage-brush just west of the bunk-house, and between it and the Headquarters Ranch House.

In an instant the whole ranch outfit was on the jump. "San Simon Dick" left his captive se-

curely hog-tied and diving behind a pile of misquite posts lost no time in returning the fire.

Presently the firing from the sage brush ceased,
and "San Simon Dick," in company with Arnold,
who had just arrived from the Ranch House with
several cowboys to take part in the battle, scouted
through the cacti and chaparal in search of the
murderer's partners.

After cautiously approaching the sage brake
they deployed and started forward. They had
advanced about twenty paces when "Bay State
Bill' stumbled over the unconscious form of a
man. They dragged him out into the level sand
and there in the clear moonlight Arnold recognized the wounded man as a former school-mate
and later treasurer of the International Development Company.

They carried him over to the corral and laid
him down beside the murderer whom he had often
befriended and shared hardship and danger in
many a reckless raid.

Colonel Cornell arrived from the Ranch House
just as the outlaw and murderer Chacon regained
consciousness. He could hardly believe his head
was in good working order, for though he knew
that Chacon would eventually be killed or captured, he never expected to see him taken alive
without some one would be riddled with lead.

Arnold, as an officer of the Arizona Rangers,
took charge of the captives and began preparations to convey them to the county jail in Tombstone in the morning, but Colonel Cornell had a
different scheme. Chacon had been tried and
convicted of robbery and murder. He was the

most wonton cruel cutthroat in the territory of
Arizona, or any other part of the southwest. He
had been convicted of murder and broke jail just
as the death penalty was about to be enforced.
What would be the effect on the rest of the cutthroats if this butcher should escape again?

Arnold kneeled down and examined the riata
which held the murderer fast. One hand was
nearly loose, but in a second Arnold had them
tied securely and as he straightened up Colonel
Cornell advanced with a lasso in hand, calling a
council of war, or as "San Simon Dick" would
put it, "they held a grand potlash," at which it
was decided to take both men and hang them to
the limb of a cottonwood tree down in the grove
near the spring, not far from the water tank.

Arnold felt sorry for his old schoolmate, but his
confession of several murders in Bisbee and his
association with Chacon left no other course, so
they were assisted to their feet, and with legs
free, hands tied behind their back and a lasso
around their necks, they were led down the creek
to the grove.

"San Simon Dick" climbed an old weather-
beaten cottonwood and carefully climbing out
about ten feet on a stout limb, tossed the rope over
a part devoid of branches and then threw the
free end to Colonel Cornell.

They were hung in different trees, for Arnold
could not see his old boyhood chum, no matter
how bad he was, hanging in the same tree with
the most heinous brute murderer who ever plied
that trade in the southwest where they have had

some very brilliant master mechanics in that line of business.

To lessen his suffering and put him out of his misery as soon as possible, Arnold had his former friend led away to another tree, and after shaking hands and biding him good-bye, he was hauled up into the limbs by the neck. Arnold, in the meantime, keeping a close guard over Chacon, not caring to witness the death of one who he had always looked on as a friend, though he had gone wrong.

Presently the men returned and as Colonel Cornell with his watch in hand gave the signal to hoist away, they all laid back and with a powerful strain, the heavy body of the outlaw was hauled up and left hanging in the tree top, while the men who had just done such a praiseworthy act in relieving the territory of such undesirable characters, returned to the Ranch House.

The news spread rapidly and two days later a coroner's jury from Bisbee, after viewing the remains, rendered the following verdict:

"We, the jury, being collected together and duly sworn, do hereby find that a 'bad man' named Chacon, who was convicted of murder, and another 'gent,' to us unknown, died of throat trouble, brought on by horse stealing, at the 'Dripping Springs Ranch' about midnight, Mexican time.

Signed: " 'Death Valley Slim,' Foreman."

CHAPTER XI.

THE CLORIDE LITERARY CLUB.

Arnold felt that the country was well rid of a pair of murderers who would stop at nothing and though he deeply regretted the miserable ending of his former schoolmate and boyhood chum, the law must be enforced and though the men had deserved their fate, Arnold gave his former friend a decent burial.

The feverish unrest of the mining district seemed to spread to the cattle country and the mines and cattle range seemed to be populated by nothing but thieves, stage robbers, rustlers, claim jumpers and all the other call loan bankers that could find their way into the country.

"San Simon Dick" came in for great praise from all hands, for it took a cool steady head to remain quiet when a murderer of Chacon's calibre was in the vicinity.

The heavy rewards were divided evenly between all engaged in the capture and the next day the whole outfit returned to Bisbee to make preparations to push forward the development of the Colonel's mines in the San Jose mountains which had turned out immensely rich since he took an interest in the claims.

Colonel Cornell was busy hiring men, buying supplies and making arrangements for the great

freight trains that were to take the place of the
pack train, which was inadapt for such a big undertaking.

Arnold and "Sam Simon," having been out in
the solitude for a long time, paid their respects to
the smoothbore hog ranch up Brewery Gulch to
hold a grand swauree and celebrate their return
to civilization, as they called it.

Harry Smith had just finished a map of the
whole group of claims, and after congratulating
his friends on their successful capture of so desperate a criminal as Chacon, they all repaired to
the opera house upon School Hill to attend a
meeting of the Bisbee Literary Club.

Some of the brightest intellectual literary lights
of the whole mining country were there and
though "San Simon Dick" sung a cowboy song,
he never took a prize, as the judges, old "Sand
Storm Cal" and Captain Hiram Danger, editor
of the Bisbee "Daily Dynamiter," said his delivery
was wanting in grace and technique, though he
was a winning bet when it came to volume and
action. As he always used the same tune for all
his songs he only had to rustle a new bunch of
words and fit them to the old tune and then let
fly.

"Jerk-line Frank" took the first prize in a trot
with his stage robber poem entitled:

"TWO BEATS ONE EVERY TIME."

"The stage rolled slowly down the trail
With its happy, merry, laughing load,
They rolled along the lizard lands

Until they struck the mountain road.
Then suddenly a voice rang out,
'Come sonny, here's the place you stop!
Don't try to pass 'till you ante up.
Get your cash ready when I say halt!
If you have no money, ther's no temptation,
So if you go wrong it's not my fault.

Climb down from that stage an' stand in line,
Eyes to the front! Hold up your hands!
My funds are low, so'ill collect a fine,
I'm a missionary from the heathen lands;
A noble work; a life divine, leading
The heathen soul o' th' rocky trail to win,
Many can help one where one cannot help
        many.
Let everybody rally 'round, and all chip in,
He covered the line with his ready gun,
And thanked each one as they paid their toll,
The same time remarking, though half in fun,
'Twas a queer collection for the heathen soul.

Gold, silver, poker chips, cards, a full deck,
As he was about to dismiss his donators,
A lass in the line requested her check,
Which she had given on his demand,
Remarking that she was a poor school-teacher,
Whereon she was challenged to play a hand
At the game which had proved his downfall.
She meekly protested she knew not the game.
He dealt out a hand. 'You ante or call,
Play for half or the whole. To me it's the
        same.'
With his gun on the line,

They sat on the robe he had thrown on the
    grass,
At the same time remarking, the weather was
    fine.
She picked up her hand, then decided to 'pass.'
He smilingly threw out the ace of the pack.
She played the two, and with a broad smile
To his utter amazement
She raked in the whole pile!
Hold there, young lady! What have you done?
The ace is a card that wins every wage.
Oh, nothing unfairly. Two always beats one.
After deep meditation and concealing his rage,
Surveying at once the length of the road,
He motioned the party to climb on the stage,
Remarking he'd hold up the very next load
And 'no school teacher poker,' said he with a
    laugh,
'From all games of chance I've forever sworn
    off.' "

It was no surprise that "Jerk-line Frank" took
first money, for he had a reputation in the "diggin's" as being a fine scholar, well able to speak
a piece, and hold his own in any language.   One
day as he was dragging along the desert with a
stage load of college professors who were out on
an expedition of deep research to try and determine "Why the jack-rabbit toes in," he fell into a
conversation with one of the learned scholars
who sat beside him on the box. Now just to
show those people he was no slouch as a Latin
scholar, he hunted over his supply for something
wise and gave them "E Pluribus Unum," "omni-

bus wagon top" and a little Latin like that, which he had learned from Dutch Baker, right off in one breath. Whoever saw a Latin scholar driving a stage coach? Well, those professors nearly dropped dead.

The next on the ledger was "Hand-Car Riley," who, carried away by his superior knowledge of Spanish, had set the requirements in rhyme for the benefit of all those who wished to qualify as a section boss in Mexico.

RAILROAD SPANISH.

Take that han' car off th' thrack,
Take that coat now off yer back,
Tomp that toi oi hov' me eye on!
Yes! What toi? Yez igrunt devil.
Line thot thrack an' make it level,
Dhrap that ile can, yah murderin' thave,
Yar th' mutive phowr on that Armstrong shivel
An' doan yez quit it without me lave.

Give an ouldher mon th' ile can,
What th' devil d' you know 'bout a car?
Yez may thravel near an' thravel far
But oim th' mon thot runs th' section,
Itchale, pronto, venneca, curry,
Thot manes move along an' hurry,
Ireva th' crowbar, poco tampo th' toi,
Ate yer dinero an' dhrink yer alkali,
Vamos th' car teh th' shoppo,
Adios, mucha grande, manana good-by.

When Riley had finished that piece Shakespeare

lost his hold on the people of the range and diggings, and the versatile section boss was crowned King of the rhymers.

The next speaker was "Heavenly Jim," the sky pilot who used to waltz up and down the streets of Tombstone, combing the toughs with a club, now and then switching in a fare-thee-well rap, that would send the wicked bad-man to the devil's reduction works in less time than a streak of lightning lasts in a storm. His effort was pretty fair and though he missed the prize by a mile he came in for a wild war-whoop of applause.

TENDERFOOT MINISTER.

He came from the East,
To look after the flock,
That made up the camp of "Pay Dirt."
Fussy and wild, guns at half-cock.
Every man in the town wore a shirt.
He had washed in the creek at "Dry Branch,"
Which was dry for the last thirty years.

In the hall at the Yellowstone Ranch,
They had heard all his heavenly pleadin's,
Some felt they should give him their pile,
Some thought that they'd give him his
    needin's.
Some said he was only a howling jack-ass.
When it came to a pinch
He'd drag out or pass.
The gamblers all 'lowed he'd be a dead cinch,
But when it came to a show down,
He was chuck full of sand,

In that little old gun game,
He could sure stand his hand.

And when the smoke cleared away,
Where they'd held the swauree
On the ground there they lay.
You could count them and see,
Six souls had lit out
For the diggin's in heaven,
While those in need of repairs
Came to thirteen times seven.

There he sat on a rock,
With his rapid fire gun,
And counted the toughs,
Who had started the fun.
This deed of destruction
He had done all alone.
For this meek little man
Had been schooled in Tombstone.

When the hurricane roar of applause had sub-
sided, Sir Edward Beecher Audney, a spruce-
looking young English mining engineer, sang a
song about "Those Dear England's Valleys and
Dales," that brought tears to the eyes of every
lad in the bunch who had ever lived on a farm.

So well was his song received that he responded
to the howl of applause by reciting that little
poem entitled, "Cousin Jack," which never fails
to bring longings to the hearts of those brave
English "chaps" who have left England's shores
in a far distant country to roam.

"COUSIN JACK."

Ah, damme ould son
I'm quittin' me haeme,
Slid out in a hurry,
I'd lik' teh gow fawster,
En fur thre' pun en six-punse
I'll be me own mawster.

In that lawnd o'er th' sea,
Ah, damme old tuss,
I'll alluz be free,
Fare better or wuss.
But th' dear little lassie,
Oh, she made such a fuss,
As I kissed 'eer gude by at th' shoremeade.
Th' dam chaps at haeme 'ill be awfter 'er tuss
Lik' mesel 'in th' valley, th' dale, en th' haem-
    steade.

Me guiding angel she alluz 'ill be,
En on earth i'm in 'eaven.
When puttin' th' tuss teh she.
An' dam th' young buggar,
Who e'er tries to hug 'er,
While I am so far o'er th' sea.

In th' far away country I roame.
Ever me dear lass she'll be.
I'm thinkin' now alluz o' haeme,
An' me dear lass so far o'er th' sea,
An' dam th' young buggar
Who e'er tries to hug 'er,
Or tries puttin' th' tuss teh she.

This recitation gave Sir Audney the lead until
"Tippearary Tige" pulled ahead with that quaint
bit of verse in which he told of his love for a lass
in the Berkshire Hills.

"SWEET BESS OF THE BERKSHIRES"

Since l'avin' that dear old Irish Isle
I'v' wandered fer money an' money a mile.
I'v' danced with th' lasses o' Clon-o-mel,
An' smiled on th' tresses o' blue-eyed Nell.
I'v' gawped at th' maidens o' gay Paree,
An' th' beauties in captive of old Turkey,
Though I'v' roamed th' world over,
On land an' on sea, I'm alluz a rover,
Of all the dear lassies that ever I see.
An' I'm sure ther's others been captured 'sides
        me ;
Yez may blow o'er th' beauty o' English Jess,
But th' queen o' them all is "Sweet Berskhire
        Bess."
Ther's mony a lad when 'es mad at a mon,
I'll up with 'es fist an' clout 'em,
But th' hardest whack yez can give a mon
Is to spake not a word about him.
An' so it is with th 'lass you love,
When she's silent an' quiet about you,
You'd rather she'd up an' hit you a clout,
Than spake not a word or doubt you.

From th' heart o' me heart I loved th' lass,
Just th' same way as she loved another.
An' I nearly drapped dead
When she breshed pass,

On th' arm o' me red-haired brother.
So I took th' hint an' flew th' coop,
To join the wild western rovers,
An' ther's mony a mon right here to-night,
Who tried drowning his sorrows
By takin' flight.
Only to find in his lonely dejection
That her charms were magnified
By the distant reflection.

As he sat on a cragg in some lonely butte,
Lazily waiting for something to shoot,
His thoughts have carried him back again,
To the lass in th' old town, he loved in vain.
Or when camped at night in th' solitude
Wild, unkept an' with manners rude,
He's thinking of his hordes of gold,
And th' dear Berkshire lassie
Only twenty years old,
Though it's twenty years since he saw her.

So then one day, 'twas
Th' same old story,
"Lonely Jim" has gone to glory.
Found in th' solitude—
Lying dead—stone dead!
He had filled his own carcass
Chuck full o' cold lead,
An' the boys looked sad
As they shuffled th' decks,
When they heard that "Jim"
Had cashed in his checks.

Of course they all 'lowed

Such an ending was hard,
For "Jim" was always
A damn good pard.
They hardly mentioned
Th' reason why,
Some said, this being
Th' mirage season,
"Lonely Jim" had
Lost his reason.
But from trials o' their own,
They knew th' story
Why "Lonely Jim"
Had gone to glory.

This recitation gave "Tippearary Tige" a big
lift in social standing. He could now waltz into
old Hankins store and demand any seat in the
place, and if suddenly taken with a fit of eloquence, he must be listened to with great respect
and attention. The customs and etiquette of the
camp demanded it, for he had drilled a good
round hole in the intellectual vein of the community, attached to fuse and when shooting time
came let her go, knocking down a big pile of pay
dirt and furnished the literary reduction works
with material enough to keep them busy for years
to come.

In a few well chosen words old Captain Hiram
Danger thanked the audience for their kind attention and appreciation of the great literary
ability of the members of the club, and just to
show them that he was no negative quantity when
it came to speaking a piece, he gave them that
little skitter entitled,

"GENTLE SALLIE."

A schoolmarm
From the East,
Did come to
Change the ways,
So wild and wolly,
Of all the wild west
Heathen kids,
And bring to time
The big town bully.

She did her work
And done it fully,
She whaled those kids,
All four times 'round.
S'lute your pardners,
She whaled 'em again,
So if they grow up
They'll walk this ground,
Like the silent
Sweet faced angel men.

She was hired
To run that school
And she was born
To lead and rule,
And after all
Those kids were whaled
None could say
That she had failed,

Oh, those kids

'Are all so tame,
They never fight
And never sass.
And now they call
A Jennie—Jane,
And a big buck mule
John Ass.

The meeting broke up, and Arnold with his
friends retired to the "Castle Rock Inn," where
they made their headquarters while in the camp.

Everything in the great Warren Mining district was on the jump. Claims were selling right
and left, and Colonel Cornell was knee deep in
business, rushing supplies and material into his
new mining camp.

The old mission workings were a bonanza, and
the great Cananea mines were pouring out copper
faster than the freighters could haul it away.

The country was overrun with toughs, bank
robbers and cattle thieves, and the Rangers had
their hands full in running down the lawless element.

Arnold had the full confidence of his employer
and did his work faithfully, and though quiet
and courteous in demeanor, and gentlemanly in
his behavior, he was always respected, and when
some unthinking "Eastern Kid" got too familiar
he firmly issued a "pronunciamento."

Colonel Cornell had bought a full water right to
all the irrigation canals along the San Pedro
River and when the profits from his mines would
allow, he bought the great San Simon Cattle

Ranch in the Huachucas and installed Albert
Arnold as foreman.

"San Simon Dick" was head of the transpor-
tation department, while Harry Smith looked
after the engineering department of the mines.

CHAPTER XII.

THE RANCH "EL SAN SIMON."

THE San Simone Ranch in the Huachucas, next to the Sierra Bonita Ranch, near Fort Grant, was the largest and best equipped in the territory, or in the whole southwest for that matter. It extended south from the southern boundary of the Fort Huachuca Military Reservation to the International Line, and from the San Pedro River on the east to the straggling Santa Cruz on the west.

So successful had Colonel Cornell been in his mining ventures, he was able to purchase vast tracts of range and ranch land, both in the territory and also in old Mexico. A few years ago he was broke. Everything seemed to be a failure with him, but he kept right at it and when he did get on his feet in the mining world, the way he took money away from the financial rubes in Wall Street was pitiable; and having a thought for the future, he invested heavily in land and cattle, and soon earned the titles of the Cattle Baron, and Copper King of the Southwest.

In selecting Arnold as foreman of his ranch, Colonel Cornell knew he had a man whom he could depend upon to do his duty. Honest and straightforward, possessed of great executive ability and brave as a lion, he felt that he could safely trust his vast cattle interests in the Ranger's hands, and depend on him to do his best to rid the country of the cattle rustlers and renegades who infested the almost inaccessable wild Sierra's and rugged plateaus along the border.

Arnold knew the whole range like a book and nearly all the people on it. He had worked in the mines and cattle range and was a very good judge of humanity and knew very well how to handle the Vaqueros and cowboys who would work under him, and though a crack shot, good rider and very accurate with the lasso, he was always gentlemanly, quiet and unassuming, and well liked by all with whom he came in contact.

After a few days' rest in town he started on the long trip to the San Simon Ranch in the Hauchucas, accompanied by "San Simon Dick," who was going to the ranch also to procure some heavy horses for his freight teams.

The first part of the trip was uneventful, and their saddle horses seemed eager to return to the range again, after being penned up in a corrol.

As "San Simon Dick" would put it, they were flying light as a July rabbit," and made good time until they came to the lonely desert station known as "Paradise Lost," a dreary supply station and watering place, about four hours' travel by saddle out on the sand waste.

The place was run by a skeleton, whose dry parched skin and hollow sunken cheeks gave him a ghost-like appearance. He had arrived at that stage where living had gotten to be a force of

habit with him and he always seemed to be there
unconcerned, movable like a sand dune on the
desert.

The inside of the station looked as if a bunch
of cowboys had been performing in twelve bar-
rooms in a night, or a government mule had
played tatoos on the interior with her hoofs. The
proprietor explained the disturbed condition of
the place by telling how two of his· guests had
engaged in a fight and an old prospector jumped
in and dusted the place with both of them.

A crazy naturalist and a loco mining expert
got into a dispute about "the evolution of the
Mexican hairless soup dog," and tried to settle
the question with the more decisive way of argument—a fight—but in so doing they stepped on
old Con Brady's toes.

Now, when a Dutchman or a Frenchman gets
mad, he is apt to kill himself, but when an Irishman gets mad he is apt to kill some one else, and
this Irishman was no exception to the rule.
When he got done with them, they were so near
dead that they could almost hear the flutter of
angels' wings, or the harsh, chilly scraping of the
devil's hoofs.

A mining expert is generally a freak cast-off of
some wealthy Eastern family who can no longer
bear to have him hanging 'round, so they get him
an appointment with some wild western mining
company in the hope that he will soon be killed
off. But he has notions of his own. When he
climbs down from the stage in "Hell Fire" Gulch
or any other gulch he loses no time in visiting the
offices of the company, but plows a trail up

through the cañon, balancing heavily from side to
side, and in his wild and wolly uniform, with his
twenty-two calibre guns tied to his frameworks,
his leggings and big hat showing up splendidly,
his "eye glawses" on, and with a poorly rolled
cigarette shoved back in his mouth, he pays his
respects to the gambling halls, and immediately
proceeds to break the bank.

The crowd gathers 'round and he becomes
reckless, sometimes betting as high as eighteen
cents, just to liven up things, and give a tone to
the occasion. Drinks are ordered and he takes a
lemonade with a straw in it.

After wiping his chops he goes at it again, he
wins. Then he loses a little, wins again, then
getting reckless he bets his whole pile and loses—
he is dead broke—rushes off to the telegraph
office, and sends the following message to his
uncle back East: "Dear Uncle, I'v' struck town
alright, she's a hummer—lots of money in sight
—everything is running full blast and our claims
are looking fine. Please send by wire five thousand dollars for development work. I start sinking a shaft to-morrow."

He is generally a graduate of some Agricul-
tural College, where he took a course in sod-cutting and hay-bailing. Now to hear him talk one
would think he knew it all, but his knowledge of
the wheel-barrow bush and the dynamite tree does
not always save him from investing in a sand pile
out on the desert.

You ask him what he thinks of the "rock" and
he will hump up his back like a mad cat and try to
look wise. Among fools he will strut around and

crow like a brave little rooster. But when in the
company of educated men he conducts himself
with an air of perpetual apology and wears on
his face an expression of everlasting resignation.

The Ranger and "San Simon Dick" were glad
to rest in the shade of a giant cottonwood tree and
paid little attention to the wrangling and quarreling of the proprietor, lounger and slowly moving
Chinaman.

It was one of those delightful, cool oases on the
trackless desert and one was loath to leave it after
traveling for hours through the sand clouds in
the vast solitude.

Presently the walking skeleton announced that
his wife had prepared a meal for all those who
could come up with the required four bits. It
was very evident that the lady of the house was
queen of the realm. She was a woman of very
decided character and in all the household affairs
she wore the garments of authority.

Now the cook seemed to have her hands full,
for in a box in the corner were a pair of twins of
about the same age and length, who were very
busy yelling at some one about a thousand miles
away, I should judge, by the way they screeched.

While they were eating the proprietor switched
in a few of his choice yarns which he had borrowed from the soldiers at Fort Huachuca. He
usually worked in a bunch of yarns to make the
meal look bigger, or just to show the people he
was no slob even if he did buy a crate of wooden
hams, and seventy-nine bushels of oats, which
proved to be wooden shoe pegs, sharpened at

both ends, or chased a razor back hog nine miles
over the desert, thinking he was going to catch a
Shetland pony.

Dinner over they went outside and "San
Simon Dick" had a smoke, all hands joining in,
as it costs nothing to smoke some one else's to-
bacco, none of the party were at all backward in
firing up. When the smoke was over and the
supply of lies had been exhausted, the proprietor
slowly dragged himself to his feet and shuffled
into a back room. Presently he emerged with a
big brown jug in his arms and as he stood on the
rickety veranda with its roof made of green cottonwood boughs, he drawled out in his inimitable
qaint and sonorous desert voice, "Any of you
fellars as wants to irrigate your system jest waltz
up 'ere and 'histe' the jug to yer heads and let
'er go. This he'ah mixture is larapin good truck,
and will sure straighten out the kinks, but don't
go too hard or you won't be able to tell which is
the butt end of a goat, or why the dog didn't catch
the jack-rabbit."

After refusing the chance to take a haul at the
jug, the Ranger and "San Simon" saddled their
horses and rode away. They made good time
across the dangerous sand waste, and that night
camped at the Indian settlement in Happy Valley, a beautiful enclosure comprising about fifteen
hundred acres of cultivated land and feeding
range for five thousand head of cattle walled in
by a natural box cañon.

The Ranger had called that way to make arrangements with the old Indian chief about the
annual round-up that was soon to take place. It

was harvest time and the Indians were showing
their appreciation to the great chief in Heaven
for the bounteous crops by holding a religious
festival.

Now the Indians, like many of their white
brethren have most of their religion in their feet,
so they were giving thanks to the Great Spirit by
holding a great dance and dog eating contest.

The Ranger and his partner looked on quietly
as the Indians whirled and howled through the
dance. Then when the dance had stopped and
the feasting began, all arrangements having been
made for the grand round-up in that part of the
country, the two horsemen rode away up the valley and out into the mesa through the narrow box
cañon on "The Big Dry" and after crossing the
rugged buttes at the west end of the Huachucas
they rode down the beautiful San Rafiel Valley to
the great ranch house "Él San Simon."

Arriving at the ranch, the Ranger was surprised to find a party of army officers and their
laides from Fort Huachuca had come to pay him
a visit. They had arrived but a short time before
the Ranger rode up and had just finished watering their saddle horses in the corral when they
saw Arnold approaching.

Captain Bruce MacGregor with his troops had
been on many a hard ride with the Rangers, after
train robbers, cattle-rustlers, smugglers and renegade Apaches, and knew the young Ranger to be
brave and generous.

The captain's brother, a brilliant young actor
from New York City, had arrived that morning
from the East, and was in search of some quiet

ranch near the fort where he could live and win back his health in the wonderful healing air of this arid region.

Of course, as the captain said, his brother could live at one of the Lunger stations out on the desert, but as a man generally lost his mind while regaining his health at those God-forgotten, lonely places, it would be much better to die in a civilized community among friends.

But the ranchers have an awful horror of the "lungers," as they call them, and generally the only way to get board at a ranch is to buy one and board yourself, for no healthy person wants a consumptive barking around him.

The Ranger knew that his employer would not have an invalid at the ranch house, but on the word of Captain MacGregor that his brother was not a consumptive, but only overworked and run down, he was given permission to live in the adobe cabin down the Arroyo at the big windmill and water tanks. The average American is a versatile man, and it does not take long to make a cowboy out of an actor. Ralph MacGregor was not only given permission to stay at the ranch, but was put on the pay roll as a full-fledged cowboy, though his duties required very little riding; he was supposed to look after the windmill and keep the ranch account books.

Captain Bruce MacGregor felt happy that he had been able to place his brother in such a good home so near the fort; and the Ranger was delighted to think he had a place to put him after he had been introduced to the charming sister,

Miss Alice MacGregor, who had accompanied her sick brother to the west.

After the arrangements were all made, the party regretting that they could not stay for supper, mounted and rode away down the trail to the fort.

"San Simon Dick" was never accused of being bashful, and when presented to the young lady fresh from civilization, he made a bow that would have crippled an ordinary man for life. As he straightened up and extended his hand, he exclaimed in wondrous admiration, "I am shoo most pow'ful glad to meet you! You are setinly the finest lookin' lady I've seen in all this yer range an' diggins."

This very frank confession from the manly young cowboy brought forth a merry laugh from the whole party, after they had recovered from their amazement at his candor.

The young lady, blushing deeply, bowed gracefully, and laughingly thanked him for his compliment so frankly given.

At that moment a commotion among the saddle horses in the corral gave "San Simon" a good excuse to retreat before further entangling himself with his confessions of admiration, and in a half bewildered way he bowed again, and nearly tumbling over himself in his excitement disappeared behind the saddle house and climbed over the fence into the corral.

The Ranger would have expressed himself just as candidly perhaps had they been alone, but under the conditions he was able to suppress any show of admiration and readily accepted the captain's invitation to accompany the party to the post and take tea at the officer's mess.

The next day Ralph MacGregor moved into his new quarters at the "tanks," and great was his surprise at the cordial reception and attendance given him by everyone at the ranch. This was a gratifying reception, indeed, for his slight cough and pallid complexion had been the cause of many a curt answer and cold stare from the haughty cattle barons and wealthy mine owners, who shunned him and avoided him as though he were a man afflicted with leprosy. One suffering with the dreaded consumption gets scant courtesy in this part of the world, and all kinds and conditions, no matter what their wealth or social position "in the States," are, out here, classed under one general term as "damned lungers."

The adventurous life of the cowboy appealed to his romantic nature. The cough soon disappeared, and the pallor on his cheeks gave way to the bronze color burnt deeply by the semi-tropical sun. The coming of this young man meant more to the gallant young Ranger than he at first anticipated. He not only had an accountant upon whom he could depend, but as foreman of the largest ranch in the southwest and his duties as a ranger, he would be away from the headquarters ranch much of the time, and in Ralph MacGregor he knew he had a man in whom he could place implicit confidence to run the ranch properly during his absence.

Miss Alice MacGregor rode up from the post every day, accompanied by the captain, to see her brother and note his progress on the slow road to recovery.

The Ranger was not slow in noticing that Miss Alice was very often accompanied by more officers than was really necessary for her safe conduct up the Government Wagon Road to the tanks and back again. "San Simon Dick" appeared to be very slow in getting down with his freight horses, and it seemed that every cowboy and vaquero on the ranch had business at the tanks when Miss Alice was supposed to be there visiting her brother.

Though not so very beautiful, all the cowboys agreed they had seen far prettier in Phoenix and Tucson. This charming young lady with a personality so winsome, so strangely elusive, vanishing, indefinable, and with a candor that won all hearts, she won the good will of all she met and many a token of love and esteem she received from the cowboys, soldiers, vaqueros and rangers, who were ready to pay homage to her charms.

Ralph MacGregor soon learned to like the desert and mountains with the open free life of a cattleman where he could enjoy the precious health regained.

His moaning and longing for one stroll along the Rialto and old Broadway, his saying that he would rather be first broom in the sweeping brigade in old New York than Governor of any State west of the Mississippi, soon changed to praise and admiration for the wild free life on the ranch and range.

His musical abilities, the key to any society, and his entertaining qualities made him very wel-

come at all the ranch jublications and swaurees
for miles around, and it was not long before his
general name of "Bones" was exchanged for the
more specific one of Mr. MacGregor.

Miss Alice MacGregor soon learned to take a
friendly interest in the manly young Ranger,
whose frank confession of some of his short-
comings at least won her respect. His reputation was first class. He had the respect and confidence of Colonel Cornell, and held a very responsible position as superintendent of his cattle
ranches. He told all about his arrest, the trial and
acquittal and also told how he was guilty and why.
The money had never been used and was still in
the Silver Bear Shaft. But it was taken out and
given to the poor forlorn lunger colony out on the
desert, where it certainly would be considered a
God-send by the poor helpless skeletons whose
prayers certainly would atone for many sins. This
done Miss Alice forgave him.

The Ranger knew very well that the young lady
fresh from the culture and refinement of the best
society in the East would feel far above him so-
cially and that this spirit of superiority would be
helped along by the jealousy and envy of many a
dashing young officer at the post.

The Ranger was equal to the occasion and con-
scious of a feeling of superiority among the society at the fort, he lost no time in noting his short-
comings and brushing up the rough places. The
blood of the best families of the old South, the
South of plantation days, coursed through his
veins, and all the honor and chivalry of his fore-
fathers exerted itself. He could easily trace his

ancestors through a line of soldiers and statesmen back to the days of Marion and Lee and the best blood of the Carolinas.

His father, a judge of the United States Land Courts for the Territories, had fought gallantly through the war as a cavalry officer under Stuart, and as he meditated and reflected on what and who he was, a certain feeling of pride and hauteur came over him and his friends on the range and at the army post were cognizant of the fact that a slight tinge of pride was noticeable in the reserved gentlemanly bearing of the stalwart young Ranger. In comparing himself with the young officers fresh from the Point, he found that he could rate himself as equal or better. His position as Lieutenant of Rangers required a man of great executive ability and cool determination, and as superintendent of the largest cattle ranch in the West he held a position of greater responsibility than many a bank president.

A man's worth will sometime or other be appreciated, and Miss Alice soon found herself interested in this manly young Southerner, who improved vastly upon acquaintance.

Affairs at the ranch were running along smoothly, and the great Spanish ranch house was the scene of many a happy gathering, enlivened occasionally by the presence of the colonel with a party of Eastern friends, to whom the scenes and incidents of ranch life were new.

The beautiful sunsets of the Santa Cruz Valley painting the country a color of gold from the romantic old Spanish mission to the wild rugged reefs and cloud-covered cliffs of the wooded chiricahuas made the place seem like a mellow Indian summer, with its smoky glowing mirage-like colors.

Miss Alice had learned to like the place, and soon found her interest in the young Ranger to be more than a passing friendship. She found out also that the cowboys, miners and ranchmen were far more afraid of her than she of them. At the ranch the life was not so lonely, and the scattered planters and stockmen had a way of getting together that was surprising to the Eastern people, who supposed there were not more than a dozen cowboys in the whole territory.

The life in the great mining cities of Tombstone, Bisbee and Cananea furnished plenty of excitement and amusement, while the novelty of the great round-up and rodero on the range and desert, the immense cattle drives and the occasional visit of some Indian chief and party made the life in this part of the world decidedly interesting.

CHAPTER XIII.

"ON THE RODERO."

THE great fall round-up had been called early in November, and vaqueros, cowboys, cattle inspectors and ranchers gathered at the Dripping Springs Ranch on the south fork of the San Pedro to take part in the big rodero. The round-up had been called later this year to avoid the fierce sand storms which blew over the great desert with unusual fury. There is nothing in the world that will stampede a bunch of cattle quicker than a sand storm, and when the vaqueros see a "blow" of unusual velocity coming they quit the herd and ride for their lives, for no horseman could hope to escape death in the terrible desert storms where tons of sand are picked up by the wind and blown with terrific fury for miles, sometimes obscuring the sun and turning daylight into darkness and burying the lonely inhabitants of the solitude in the shifting drifts.

It was supposed that the storms had all passed, and the ranchmen looked forward to a successful "drive." Great herds were gathered and "held" in the valley while the "cutting-out" was going on. The beef were corraled and kept in a separate bunch by the herd guard while the "feeders"

were turned loose on the range again. The
Mavericks and "strays" were equally divided
among the cattle owners, and after all were
branded, and some were so thoroughly covered
with hieroglyphics that their sides looked like the
mysterious carvings on a slab of Acztec stone calendar, they were turned loose on the mesa.

The great round-up was about half over, when
there arrived at the ranch a young man from the
East, who had quit his college career after spending three years in the freshman class.

Colonel Cornell had met his father in Wall
Street, and evidently thinking to place his son out
of reach of all temptation, he sent him to the
Colonel's ranch out here in the wilds of Arizona
to live a quiet saintly life with the gentle cowboys.

Three years in the freshman class and taking
the course in sod-cutting at that, then comes out
here to take a post-praduate course in bronco riding and mule driving, he finally winds up with
M.D. hitched onto his name.

M.D. stands for mule driver, and as all men
cannot have degrees fired at them by college facul-
ties, it is a good way to acquire one.

Colonel Cornell gave the young man a cordial
welcome, and as a party of officers, with their
ladies from the post, had just ridden up, they all
repaired to the corrals to see the branding and
also to see a college cowboy get his first lesson in
the gentle art of breaking broncos.

This college cowboy had plenty of sand and
had won a great fame as a football player, so to
the surprise and amazement of all the bronco

busters he walked into the corral and called for
his first lesson. A powerful looking mountain
mustang was led out of the bunch, and after
about two hours of choking and dragging a big
double cinch saddle was cinched in place, and the
world renowned half-back climbed into the seat.
The terrified bronco had seen very few men in his
life, and then only when they caught him, and
after having his wind knocked out by being
bounced around the desert on the end of a lasso,
a red-hot iron burned several figures into his
hide.

All broncos go pretty strong on the eleventh
commandment—"Don't get caught"—and they
try to follow the twelfth, which reads: "Break
your captor's neck." Well, they all try faithfully
enough, and this one was no exception. Just as a
starter he shot that half-back up into the clouds
and belted him twice with his hoofs before he
reached the earth again. Now a football player
is a hard animal to kill, and this one gathered
himself, and shouting, "Never mind the time
out," started for his bronco again. In vain did
the vaqueros try to dissuade him, for in his weakened condition he might be killed. Talk went for
nothing and the horse was caught again, and to
the utter amazement of the spectators the mustang could not shake him out of the saddle, though
of course he "choked" leather, but that was ex-
cusable in a tenderfoot.

A bronco knows his business when it comes to
getting rid of a tenderfoot, and after snorting and
plunging around the corral in a desperate endeavor to throw the stubborn rider, the terrified

animal reared up and fell over backward, pin-
ning the unlucky fellow underneath. A wild
shout of amazement went up from the spectators
at the corral gate, for they thought he had been
crushed to death.

Cowboys, vaqueros, army officers and ranchmen vaulted the adobe wall and ran to his assistance, but their services were not required. The
wild bronco had regained his feet, and crossing
the corral in five jumps cleared the corral gate
like a bird, scraping the saddle off against the top
cross-bar, jumped over the smoke house and lit
out over the plains for his feeding grounds in the
mountains.

Half the ladies in the party had fainted, and the
whole ranch was thrown into wild confusion by
the awful accident in the corral, but when the
horse released him the half-back arose slowly to
his feet, and after digging the sand out of his
mouth and eyes announced himself as ready for
another go.

The post surgeon examined him thoroughly
and found no broken bones, and not even a bruise.
The cowboys and ranchmen looked on in wondrous amazement, while the half-back was "trying
out" his legs and arms to satisfy himself that he
was all there.

He treated the affair with supreme contempt,
and nearly killed all the cowboys by throwing out
a few remarks about turning left-end for ninety
yards with ten players on his back.

The college cowboy made good right on the
kick-off, and the boldest vaquero on the ranch
would not think of addressing him as "The Ten-

derfoot" or any other title implying greenness,
and it was a stand-off with the cowboys whether
or not his hide would turn bullets.

That night he was the hero of the cotillion
given at the ranch house, and the way he glided
over the floor one would never suspect that a wild
outlaw bronco had battered his frameworks and
bounced him around on the desert. Indeed, Sir
Harry Hicks agreed that he was the best speci-
men of indestructability he had ever met, and Sir
Harry had travelled some, for his occupaton as a
mining engineer took him into all parts of the
world, and a better judge of human nature never
drifted into this end of our cowboy republic. A
word from Sir Harry went a long way among the
people of the range and diggings, for whatever
his title in England all the ranchmen and cowboys
here voted him to be a prince among men and a
natural born gentleman.

Dancing ceased at the great rambling ranch
house while the guests assembled on the veranda
to watch the signal fires that burned brightly on
the high promontory in the dragoon mountains far
across the valley. Presently the peaks at Fort
Grant lit up, and the great butte known as
"Cochise stronghold" was reflecting the danger
signal to all the settlers in the valley and desert
below. Signal fires could be seen burning on the
shelf of the great exposed reef in the mountains
back of Fort Huachuca.

Three fires burnt brightly on each peak, that
the settlers in the valley and on the desert might
seek safety from the terrible sand storm that was
sweeping down the San Simon Valley from the

great white sand wastes on the north. The authorities at the posts had received the warning,
and the signal corps lost no time in notifying the
cattlemen, prospectors and all who might be
caught in its way.

There was great commotion at the ranch. Cowboys were saddling their mounts, and every one
who could ride was pressed into service to try and
hold the great herds during the sand storm which
evidently would be of unusual fury, for the distant bugle calls at the post told plainly that the
cavalry troops were falling in and forming in
squads ready to patrol the desert and rescue anyone unfortunate enough to be overcome by the
terrific "blow" that sometimes buried whole cattle outfits under tons of soft snow-white sand, and
piling up on the lonely desert stations left the
country white and level with not a single trace of
former habitation.

The lights burned brightly on the mountain
tops, and in the intense darkness shone like solitary stars in the heavens. A terrific rumbling
could be heard far up the valley, and as the sound
of the awful roar grew plainer the great herds of
wild cattle in the valley became restless, and the
vaqueros found it a dangerous task trying to hold
them.

A bunch of wild horses in the big branding
corral were running around and surveying the
wall for a favorable place to escape. A big white
mule was turned into the corral to see if the presence of a calm leader would have any effect in
quieting them, for it is a well-known fact that
horses will follow the example of a mule when

they feel that danger is near. A mule is a very wise animal, and will not take fright unless there is danger near. This old mule had been on the desert for many years and never took part in a stampede until the big "blow" of " '86," when a whole pack train and two companies of scouts were buried in a furious storm that swept down the San Simon Valley. The tough old mule was the only animal, brute or human that came out of the big storm alive.

Evidently her presence in the corral had the desired effect on the frightened herd, for they quieted down and seemed satisfied that there was no danger.

The burning winds that blew down the valley were almost unbearable, and as they increased in velocity, picking up sand as they went, the cowboys and vaqueros found it nearly impossible to hold their positions and keep the herds in check.

The terrific rumble and roar of the hurricane as it rolled down the valley, carrying tons upon tons of dry, shifting sand, could be plainly heard at the great ranch house, and the ladies in the party knelt and prayed that the mercy of God would be shown to all those who might be caught in its fury.

The night was so dark that the cowboys could not see a foot ahead, and as the cattle had grown more restless and occasionally a crazy steer would dart out from the herd, the ranger gave orders to set fire to the big hay stacks near the corral, so they could see to hold the terrified "bunch." The attraction of the blaze seemed to have a quieting effect upon the herd, and the cowboys began to

hope that they would not stampede, but just as everything began to look favorable a flash of lightning lit up the whole valley, followed by a terrific crash of thunder that seemed to jar the whole earth and send its echoes around the world as the violent cannonading rolled from peak to peak and roaring in the dismal cañons made it seem that the planets were battering into each other.

At the first flash of lightning the old white mule let one long snort, threw up her tail and sailed over the adobe wall like a bird and tore away down the valley, followed by every crazy bronco in the corral.

The herd had been waiting for a leader, and as the mule pounded along past the terrified steers threw up their tails and fell in behind. The whole tornado of hoofs and horses, sand and cattle rolled on down the valley, storming along over the desert, carrying death and destruction as they rolled over or slammed into everything that stood in the way.

As Arnold saw the white mule jump the corral fence, he drew his six-shooter, and fired three shots as a signal for the cowboys and vaqueros to ride for their lives to escape the roll of hoofs and horns sweeping down on them. The great stampede was on, and as the storm broke in wild terrific fury it buried whole herds of cattle in its course as the stifled animals soon fell exhausted in the suffocating sand.

Signal guns at Fort Huachuca could be heard in the lull of the storm as they boomed out their warning to those poor unfortunates who might be caught on the desert in that awful tornado of sand.

As the warning signal blazed out from Arnold's gun, the vaqueros wheeled their horses and rode for the side of the valley to escape the wild plunging herds as they reared and stormed along down the coast. The tornado was blowing with terrific velocity, and the herd guard had barely reached the friendly shelter of the great ranch house when the heavens opened, and amid incessant flashing of lightning and constant crashing of thunder, cloudburst after cloudburst flooded the valley, and the smoky old volcano up near Antelope Pass began its awful coughing, and as each effort shook the very earth it seemed that daylight would reveal a country more desolate than the dreary death valley out in the great sand wastes on the Colorado.

Nothing could be done until daylight, for there was great danger of being trampled to death if any horseman ventured out on the plains while a general stampede was on.

The great rain storm would probably check the stampede, for nothing will bring a bunch of cattle to their senses quicker than wading through a vast field of mud.

Towards morning the storm had passed the herds and swept on down the valley, and as day broke over the mesa and pampas great numbers of horses and cattle could be seen stuck in the mud all over the valley and plains. As the ground dried, and under the fierce rays of the southern sun it dries very quickly, the animals have little difficulty in releasing themselves, but occasionally a steer or horse exhausted by a long run is too weak to move, and then unless dragged out of his mud bed by some vaqueros he is sure to die from thirst and starvation.

Many members from the officers' party from the post had never witnessed a "blow" on the desert before, and the roar of the storm and pounding and clashing of hoofs and horns as the frightened herds stampeded over the valley made a scene awful enough to strike terror to the stoutest heart.

As Arnold reached the ranch house after firing the signal to abandon the herd, he found Miss MacGregor in a great worry about her brother, who would be in great danger at the tanks if a cloudburst should sweep down the high-walled cañon.

To venture into the cañon on such a night would be courting death, but the young man must be warned of his danger, as Eastern people know very little about the ways of these storms in these rugged cañons and valleys.

The Ranger made his way on foot to the tanks, and as he drew near the cozy little cabin, he could see young MacGregor reading by the light of a huge Spanish lamp, and seeming utterly indifferent as to the conditions the foul weather had produced.

Arnold began to whistle as he approached the hut, that his presence might become known without any sudden jar to the nerves of the occupant. He had descended the bank and started to cross the "dry wash" when the young actor appeared in the doorway to greet him.

The tanks were sheltered from the desert winds by the high cliffs and buttes along the cañon in the dip of the mesa, so MacGregor had felt none of the storm's severity, though he was very well aware of its devastation in other parts.

Arnold informed the young actor of the danger of staying in the cañon during a severe storm, for the system of draining the rain clouds in the wild rugged mountains of Arizona is a little different to that employed in more civilized parts.

There are no showers or drizzling rains, but when the clouds find a convenient place they open up and drop whole rivers of water down on the mountains and deserts, filling the cañons and "washes" with a raging torrent that rolls along with a front wall from four to fifty feet high and sweep everything in its way.

They locked up the cabin and started across the "draw" and had nearly reached the center, when the Ranger's practised ear caught the particular rapid surging sound of a cloudburst rushing down the "draw." Arnold gave a warwhoop loud enough to put speed into any tenderfoot, and the actor made a leap and shot up the bank to safety. The Ranger was not quick enough, being hampered by heavy riding boots, "chaps" and a long "saddle slicker," and as he caught at the brush on the side of the cañon the full breast of water, six feet high, struck him, and in an instant he was being carried down the arroyo to what seemed certain death.

Being a powerful swimmer he managed to stay up for a short while, but the riding boots were exhausting his strength and the storm coat inter-

fered with his movements. He went down twice
in the raging torrent of muddy water, and just
as his strength was nearly gone a brilliant flash
of lightning lit up the whole country. A wild
bronco was swimming past him and with one desperate effort the half-drowned Ranger grabbed
his mane and climbed on his back. Though the
seat was uncomfortable it beat swimming, and
with a thought for the future Arnold threw off his
oil coat and kicked off his boots to prepare himself for another swim and make navigation more
feasible. Securely seated on the hurricane deck
of the bronco, he swept down the raging stream,
making steamboat time. The raging torrent was
full of dead cattle, driftwood and big cottonwood
trees that swept down, turning end over end and
making life decidedly unsafe for anyone floating
around in the way.

The bronco chugged and snorted, and half
frightened to death made wild plunges to shake
off the rider, but the ranger hung on, and as they
surged under a big cottonwood Arnold made a
desperate leap, and grabbing an overhanging
bough easily hauled himself up into the limbs to
safety and climbing across the rocky ledge he
hauled off his clothes and wrung them out.

He had been in the water scarcely five minutes,
but in that time had drifted down stream nearly
three miles. It would be hard work to walk back
to the ranch, but the ranchers would be searching
for him and beating the bush, and climbing along
the dangerous rim of the cañon in the darkness
was no picnic.

He sat on a ledge and rested. Presently the

terrific crashing and rolling of thunder ceased, and the cloudburst having drained the heavens the water in the cañon began to recede, and in fifteen minutes the raging torrent had passed and the cañon was as dry as though Arizona had been enjoying one of her seven-year dry spells.

The Ranger climbed down the rugged wall and walked up the cañon bed towards where the tanks had been. He knew the searchers would scout along the creek for his body as soon as the flood had passed, and hoping to meet them he held his course to the creek bed. As he rounded the promontory near the ruins of the cliff dwellers he saw a signal fire burning on a high peak in the buttes back of the ranch.

Evidently the army officers were signalling with fire, for being familiar with the code he could easily read the message being sent to the fort, which read: "Ranger drowned—scout cañon." Hoping to relieve their anxiety, he drew his six-shooter from the holster and fired three shots in the air as a signal that all was well. As the gun flashed a great mountain lion that had been tearing at the carcass of a young steer sprang at him and buried its teeth and claws in his shoulder as he fell to the ground. He shot the animal dead, but not until it had nearly torn off his arm. He lay in the soft sand and waited, but no help came. His ammunition all gone, he put his uninjured hand to his mouth and gave the call of the cowboys and rangers that is used only when in great distress. He raised on his elbow and thought he could hear the distant bugle calls of the cavalry, but as he listened he knew he could hear the far-away neighing of his saddle horse away up in the foothills.

Treat a horse kindly and he will stay with you in all kinds of weather. If you are kind to him he will answer your call of distress, and if possible will come to your aid. The Ranger had always been kind to his saddle horse, often his sole companion for weeks while running cattle out in the strange and dreary solitude, and as he called again he was answered by his pony galloping up the bed of the cañon. With a friendly neigh of recognition the intelligent animal ran to him and began nibbling at his coat pockets for the biscuit that was generally there for him. Arnold caught the bridle reins that was trailing on the ground, and with great difficulty climbed into the saddle and rode slowly up the cañon to the signal fire.

The ranchers and cowboys had given up all hope of finding him alive, and when those about the blaze saw him ride out of the darkness they were wild with joy, and piling on more wood began firing signals for the searchers to return.

As they approached the great ranch house they could see the people gathered in the parlor, and as Arnold stepped into the room, Miss Mac-Gregor, who was nearly hysterical at the thought of his death, thanked him profusely for risking his life to save her brother, and commended him on his great courage and bravery.

The Ranger, overcome by exposure, apologized for his weakened condition, and after explaining the cause of his sudden collapse received the congratulations of all hands around for his daring adventure in the cañon.

The post surgeon dressed his torn shoulder, and in two days Arnold was able to join the round-ups and help in the "cutting-out process," going on at the Rangers' camp out in the San Simone Valley. To avoid disputes the Rangers took charge of all the cattle gathered after the great stampede, and as each brand was "cut out" the owner drove the whole outfit away to his own ranch.

The line riders along the border had great difficulty turning the wild herds during the tornado, and many cattle crossed the border into Mexico. Then the rustlers got busy and did a paying business in selling beef to the mining camps in the state of Sonora across the Mexican line.

Arnold with a troop of Rangers and Colonel Kosterlitzsky with three troops of Mexican Rurales started out to capture the whole bunch before they could escape into the wild rugged Yaqui Indian country, where pursuit would be impossible.

CHAPTER XIV.

CATTLE RUSTLERS ALONG THE BORDER.

CATTLE rustlers are hard customers to catch, and the line riders along the border were unable to hold the smugglers in check, not speaking of the other class of outlaws who crossed and re-crossed the line at will.

Chasing cattle thieves is no picnic in this end of the world, and the Rangers realized the great danger and hardship to be met in a campaign against the renegades.

Word was brought by an Indian courier that a band of rustlers were camped up on "The Big Dry" in the Cananea Mountains, and Colonel Kosterlisca with his Rurales had them surrounded and was waiting for the Rangers to come up and hold the lower pass, where the Silver Creek trail crossed the Indian Reef up into the wild buttes and mountain peaks.

One man could hold the pass against a regiment, and after posting two Rangers there Arnold deployed his men and scouted through the east side of the basin, while the Rurales beat the bush on the west side.

The men had dismounted and were crawling slowly through "the brake" when the sharp, shrill

whistle of a bullet was heard as it whizzed by
their heads.

Now the only way to fight outlaws is to fight
them Indian fashion, and as that bullet whizzed
past every man ducked for cover and crawled
along in concealment. There being no report
heard, it was evident that the shot came from a
high power rifle on the far wall of the basin.

The ranger is too good a scout to be caught in
a trap, and Arnold, knowing well that the shot
was only a blind to draw him away, sent word to
Colonel Kosterlisca to scout through the buttes
where the shots came from, while he continued to
search the basin.

They had not gone far when the Indian guide
came hurrying back with the information that the
outlaws were camped in a narrow box cañon,
where they were holding a big bunch of stolen
cattle.

A hurried council of war was held, and it was
decided to surround the camp and take the outlaws alive if possible, as they were all seated by a
camp fire and eating their noonday meal, evidently
not suspecting any trouble.

Arnold crept slowly through the sage brush
and worked his way noiselessly along the rim of
the cañon and hid in a clump of grease wood, not
thirty feet away from the robbers.

Evidently the rustlers did not think there was
any danger of pursuit, for they had posted but
one guard up on the Indian Watch, a high peak
overlooking the valley and at one time used by
the Apaches as a signal station while sending up
their smoke signs.

Arnold could hear every word that passed among the men as they lounged around the camp fire and reviewed past raids. They were discussing the train robbery that took place out in the valley near Douglas.

"I guess that trick will fool them all right," remarked a tall, swarthy-looking young fellow as he slowly rolled a cigarette. "I 'low the whole Ranger force and all the sheriffs in the territory are scouting the desert and mountains out in the Chiricahuas and Swisshelms with a notion of catching the train robbers."

"Well," continued the speaker as he lit his cigarette against a coal, "we'll have no trouble in driving this bunch across the line, and when we reach Guymas, I'm off to Chili on the first ship. I don't think we can afford to lose much time, for when the Rangers find out that the train hold-up was a one-man job they will ride straight for these mountains and make it too hot for the rustlers."

"This is my last raid, and if I'm successful I'm off to another country. I know Arnold, and when he gets on your trail there's no let up until you're caught."

"Th' hell, you say," broke in a short, heavy set man who was laying on his back gazing at the stars. "Kid, you're losing your nerve. You'd ought to bin with us in that fight with the Yaquis. There ain't many fellers left of that raid. Let me see, we killed some Chicago mining men and got a good swag, but they wiped out a few of our gang. 'Yellowstone Bill' died of throat trouble after he got his lasso tangled up with another

man's cattle. Pat Barrett nearly wiped out all the
rest in a big fight up on the Animas River, two
more were filled with lead up in Tonto Basin.
Well, I 'low, me an' 'Red Horse Mike' is the only
representatives of that noble band left."

"Speakin' of that damned Ranger, I captured
him one night out on the desert, but he slipped the
bridle off his horse's head and rode away in a
storm of lead. Can't see how we missed him, but
he was never touched."

Arnold listened attentively as the outlaws rehearsed old raids and murders they had been
mixed up in.

Presently a tall, swarthy Mexican vaquero
rode up to the camp, and a heavy-set cutthroat
who had been laying on the ground arose and saddled a powerful looking saddle horse.

After thoroughly inspecting the cinches and
refilling his canteen he drew a carbine from under a roll of blankets, and after carefully loading
it placed it in the saddle scabbard, then after a
short conversation with the Mexican, who was
seated on a blanket, eating mountain oysters, he
swung himself into the saddle and rode slowly
into the box cañon to take his place as herd guard
over the bunch of stolen cattle.

From what he could see and hear the Ranger
concluded that there were five men in the bunch,
and slowly retreating to "the brake" which the
Rangers and the Rurales had designated as a
rendezvous, he sent four men to capture or, if
necessary, kill the herd guard, while he with six
men would rush the camp and capture the whole
outfit.

Arnold had invaded the outlaws' stamping grounds with the intention of capturing or killing every thief in the region, for since the opening up of the great bonanza mining circle in the Bisbee Basin the country had become overrun with thieves and cutthroats, who, too lazy to work, took very readily to the easy methods of the International Beef Forwarding Association, as the rustlers are known here in polite society.

These robbers would steal cattle in Arizona and drive them through the passes of the Huachuca Mountains down into the state of Sonora and sell them at the towns and mining camps. Then after a slight rest they would make a midnight raid on some mining camp, and before morning came they were safe in the caves and cañons of the wild and rugged Huachucas in Arizona.

Evidently the outlaws felt secure, for they were all seated on a blanket playing cards, except the Mexican who had rolled up in his blankets and was snoring lustily.

Five rifles rested against a log and each man at the card game had two six-shooters in his belt.

Arnold and his squad of rangers worked their way noiselessly to the edge of the brush, and at a given sign each man arose and covered an outlaw with his rifle before he could move.

The robbers knew the penalty of an attempt to pull a gun, and in an instant they were all disarmed and securely tied.

The guard up in the box cañon was too good a scout to be caught asleep, and as his horse threw up its head and surveyed the cañon ridge he knew someone was approaching, and quickly swinging his ca. bine into line sent a bullet through a hat as its owner dodged behind a shelf of rock. The guard slid off his horse and dodged behind a big ledge, but not quite quick enough to escape the bullet that a Ranger had sent after him.

The bullet plowed through his shoulder, and when the Rangers came up they found him unconscious in the soft sand wash of the creek bed.

After disarming him he was placed on a blanket and carried to the camp where the other prisoners lay securely tied.

A report of a carbine rang out through the clear mountain air, and presently a general firing could be heard, not the measured discharge as of soldiers in battle, but the continual fusilade of bushwhackers and cattle runners as they engaged in their favorite mode of guerilla warfare.

Leaving a guard to watch the prisoner, Arnold hurried away to the scene of fighting.

Cattle were straying away from the herd, there being no one to guard them, whereon the Ranger sent a man to hold the bunch, and continuing on down the valley, joined the main body of Rangers who were keeping up a steady fire apparently at the rocks and cliffs in the rugged buttes along the cañon.

The Ranger had lived on the desert during the fierce Apache wars and knew exactly how the troops of Miles and Lawton used to fight the wily old Geronimo.

Under the fierce glare of the southern sun the men in the bottom of the cañon were at a great disadvantage in returning the fire of the renegades up in the buttes, for the glare of the sun

shining on the rifle barrels made it nearly impossible to do any accurate shooting, and accurate
shooting is a great requisite to the Ranger if he
has any notions of dying of old age.

Now the Arizona Rangers are by far the greatest bunch of horsemen in the world, and as bushwhackers and guerilla fighters they can easily
make the wild Indian look like a mud fence when
it comes to fattening the earth by the graveyard
route.

The word was quickly passed for every man to
keep under cover and skirmish along the cañon to
the old Spanish ore trail and cross up into the
buttes above the Yaqui Indians and renegades
and keep up an infalading fire.

The order was quickly executed, and as the
Rangers scouted along through the rugged buttes
they could see Kosterliscas Rurales on the right
and above the renegades, thereby cutting them off
from all chance of escape.   \

Their ammunition was giving out, and knowing
very well that if they surrendered they would be
taken to Arispe and shot, they made a wild charge
in a desperate attempt to rush the pass.

The country was rough and broken, and as the
brave Yaqui chief led the charge he was shot
down before he had made ten jumps towards the
hope of escape.

At the sight of their fallen chief the Yaquis lost
heart and all surrendered. Several Rangers had
been wounded, but a Ranger, as I said before, is
a past master at the art of bushwhacking, and to
plunk his carcass in a vital part is a hard trick to
turn.

The Rurales, being old timers at the killing game, lost but four men, though many were badly wounded.

At a council of war it was decided to camp in the cañon that night, as the danger of an attack was very slight and as the wandering bands of smugglers are not prowling around looking for a scrap with the line riders or Rangers, there would be little danger from that source.

The captives were all driven into a narrow cave, and as night came on great fires were built so that the guards at the entrance could see to shoot any one that might try to run the gauntlet in a desperate attempt to get away, for they all knew very well that if they ever reached a Mexican judge they would be stood up against a wall and filled full of lead.

Arnold picked out a few prisoners who had done some robbing in Arizona and tied them up with his bunch of renegades.

All the peaks and passes were well guarded, and feeling safe in their high-walled cañon the Rangers staked out their saddle horses that had been led up after the battle, and while some sat around the camp fires telling yarns of wild adventure in the Yaqui country others were busy taking care of the wounded, who seemed to be suffering great pain.

To the stranger happening along it would seem that the Rangers' camp was a place for recreation instead of a hurried bivouac in the rustlers' country. But though the camp was strewn with saddles and rifles, blankets and gun holsters, sombreros and riding boots, gauntlets and bridles, it would be a revelation to the tenderfoot to see how quickly these vaqueros could arm and stand off the wildest charge the Yaquis could make, and it is freely admitted by all who have done any fighting in the wild that a Yaqui Indian is a fierce devil when he gets started.

All that night the fires were kept burning brightly, and though the long southern gloom was made hideous by the continual howling of coyotes up in the buttes and peaks there was no attack, and early the next morning, and morning in the southwest comes about three o'clock, they all saddled up and broke camp, the Rurales departing for Sonora with their Indian prisoners, while the Rangers took charge of five much-wanted rustlers and smugglers who would undoubtedly get a lift in society by being raised gently up into the limbs of a cottonwood as soon as they reached Tombstone, if not sooner.

The Lieutenant of Rangers was no Sunday school boy, and had never grown bald-headed over worry brought on by indulging in a draw game where the object of the sport was a cutthroat swinging at the end of a lasso, but other people must be taken into consideration, and knowing very well that he would be looked upon with horror and disgust by a young lady at the fort whose affections he had partly won if he took these outlaws and hung them without a formality of a jury trial, he decided to take them to Tombstone and let the grand jury take a fall out of them at the next term of court.

Arnold learned from the prisoners that the herd of cattle had been stolen at the turkey-track ranch and was to be driven to Magdalena and sold to the Mexican cattle drivers.

The Yaqui Indians had terrorized the country and would find little difficulty in getting the herd across the line and past the mines of Cananea.

It is against the law to sell or give firearms to the Yaquis, but this bunch had a habit of smuggling opium and mescal across the border and exchanging their plunder for rifles, ammunition, cattle and horses that the rustlers and smugglers gathered on the Arizona side.

The line riders took charge of the stolen cattle and drove them away to the big corral at the custom house in Naco.

Colonel Kosterlisca marched his captives to Arispe, where the judge of the first instance, after a trial lasting about ten minutes, sentenced them to death.

That night at sundown the Yaquis were all lined up against the adobe wall of the fort and furnished good target practice for the Rurales, who shot every one of them dead. It's rather sudden, but that's the way they have of doing business in this end of the world.

The Rangers tied their prisoners each on a horse, and with two scouts leading the way, the rustlers in the middle and the rest of the troop bring up the rear, the party followed the trail down past the old abandoned silver smelter and on through the Arroyo seco until they came to the camp of a prospector, where they stopped and watered their mounts and ate a lunch generously funished by the kind-hearted old wandering miner.

Well knowing their fate, the cutthroats had very little appetite for the meal so welcomed by the Rangers, and even the short, thick-set man, who had been so brave in camp with his pals, was now in a very gloomy frame of mind, though perhaps his wound might be the cause of his great depression.

The old prospector seemed troubled with a great grief, and calling Arnold aside they walked slowly up the creek bed to the spring, where the old man began to explain the formation of rock in the face of a drift he had driven in the side of the cliff, where a true fissure vein could be traced in the rich gold-bearing ledge at the blow-out.

The old miner took some rock from an old powder box and began explaining how the vein pitched and how high it would run in gold. Arnold was well enough acquainted with this quaint and strange class of people to know that this was only the prelude to some great secret that he was about to divulge, and had not long to wait. After surveying the cañon with a slow, searching eye, the old man began:

"Young man, you're frum the South?"

"Yes, suh," replied the Ranger slowly, "I'm a Southerner."

"Well," continued the old man, "I don't know as I need to make any apologies, but a friend uv mine—an' he's a black man—was killed near the post yesterday mawnin'. Now, mind, I never looked on him as a nigger, but just as a black man, same as you're a white man. No offence now, but he wuz th' squarest man I ever met, an' he's grubstaked me many a time. When luck

wuz agin me an' he sez, sez he, Hogan, sez he,
never mind, you'll strike it yet, an' if y'u don't
I've got enough fur both uv us.

"I don't know you, young feller, but I've hearn
y'u spoke uv. Now th' men that killed '·'Nigger
Ned' wuz rustlers and smugglers, an' they killed
him for a dam'd pinch of gold, an' stole a few
maps, an' 'Malachite Mike' wuz found up at the
spring near Soldiers' Gardens with four bullet
holes in his head. I exchanged shots with 'Malachite' one day over in Tombstone, but we'v allus
been good friends, an' now I want yer permission
to quietly kill the last man you got in that bunch."

As the Ranger listened to the story he slowly
sank to the ground, and resting on his boot heels
picked up a small rock and began drawing lines
in the earth with it and seemed lost in study.

He had made no answer to anything the prospector said, but listened as though the man was
putting forth an every-day proposition in the line
of a horse trade.

Evidently he was lost in deep meditation, for
he paid no attention to the old miner, and as a
Ranger called from down the cañon he arose and
walked slowly to the camp.

The Ranger was in a terrible stew, for he was
very well aware that if he hung his prsoners he
would be looked upon as a brute by Miss Mac-
Gregor, who did not approve of the strenuous
way in which bad men are dealt with in this end
of "the big sand."

He had often been befriended by "Nigger
Ned" and old "Malachite" and would gladly take
the outlaws and kill the last one of them with his

own gun, but by so doing he knew he would lose the love and esteem of one who was all the world to him.

He knew if they were found guilty and hung by due process of law he would be regarded as an honorable brave man and a dashing young hero by the lady whose winning ways had won his heart. But though an awful crime had been committed and his dearest friends brutally butchered for a few dollars, he well knew that if he took the law into his own hands or permitted his men to do so, he would be avoided as a bloodthirsty ghoul by the young lady who had learned to love him.

As they neared the camp the Ranger turned to the prospector and cautioned him not to mention the murder to the troopers, for if those horsemen became aware of the crime committed by their prisoners, they would burn them alive.

Parties of ranchmen and cowboys, soldiers and prospectors would scout the desert and mountains for the murderers, when the crime became known, and all the rangers and soldiers in Arizona would not be able to prevent a lynching if the cutthroats were captured.

It was twenty-eight miles to Tombstone and seven miles of that a hot shifting desert trail. Any party leaving the watering places and venturing out on the shifting sand waste would do so at great risk, for the mirage season was on and the gloom of the solitude had settled in the great lone stillness.

CHAPTER XV.

IN THE GREAT SAND AND SOLITUDE.

THE Ranger knew very well if he took the rustlers and hung them he would win the approval of nearly every cattle man and mine owner in the solitude, but there was another great influence brought to bear and cause him to determine to land his prisoners in jail, no matter what obstacle stood in the way.

He had never been told, but still he knew exactly how he would be loathed by one in the community whose good will and esteem he much preferred above all the rest.

Calling the Rangers he quietly told them of the hard task on hand and appealed to each horseman to stand by him, no matter what should come.   The appeal was unnecessary, for these wild riding horsemen are true as steel.

At the call to mount the rustlers were all securely tied on horseback, and at the order to "drag it" from the captain, each Ranger leisurely swung to the saddle and took his place in line or rear guard, as was directed.

The horsemen rode rapidly down the trail, and when they reached a friendly turn in the deep cañon that shut off the view from old Hogan's cabin, they followed the trail up into the mountains, intending to cross the San José Mountains and take the trail out by the old mission, across the wild mesa, and go out over the desert by the southern trail, where trading posts and desert stations were not quite so scarce, as they are on the great sand route.

The Rangers were hardly out of the cañon when old Hogan, the grizzled old prospector, mounted his big white mule and rode out on the range to spread the news among the cattlemen and cowboys who were on the rodero.

The wild war cry rang through the range and ranch, and the call of the cowboy could be heard wherever the cattle roamed, and for the first time in twenty years great clouds of signal smoke went up from the mountain peak "Indian Watch" in the Huachucas.

This signal is used only when a raid by Indians or outlaws is expected or some awful murder has been committed at a lonely ranch or desert station in the solitude.

Knowing very well that the ·old pospector would spread the alarm, the ranger captain had chosen the southern trail to avoid the cowboys and ranchmen whom he knew would swarm over the desert and through the mountains by the old government trail leading to the fort.

The horses had seen hard service, and the rocky cow path made the going still slower. It was the time of the mirage on the desert and electric storms in the mountains, and a forced march across this rugged country, beset by outlaws and storms in the mountains and enraged cowboys and sand storms on the desert, made it a very difficult task to cross the waste.

The trail became so rough that the Rangers had to dismount and walk. They picked their way slowly around the rugged "grey horse butte" and crossed the lower branch of Antelope Creek, where they stopped at the cabin of an Indian hunter, who fed them and gave Arnold a map of the trail that would be of great help.

The Indian warned him against the dangers that beset any traveller who undertook to cross the mesa, as it swarmed with outlaws and rustlers who had been driven out of Mexico by the Rurales.

After a short rest the horsemen moved on, and by sundown they had made the "Troopers Rest Springs," at the mouth of the cañon that leads up to the mission.

The men were only too glad to rest, and dismounting they pitched camp on the rise just west of the tank of clear water, where they could easily repel any attack that they rightfully expected would be made by friends of the rustlers during the night. The horses were turned loose, and after the rustlers were securely tied to the wheel of an old abandoned freight wagon the men arranged camp for the night and began preparing supper.

Antelope were very plentiful, and "Berkshire Bill," the best shot among the Rangers, brought one into camp after being away but a few minutes.

Instead of trying to conceal their presence, the Rangers lit a big camp fire to give the impression that they were prospectors out on a search for gold. The trick might work and it might not, but in their worn out condition the horsemen were willing to run the risk that they might enjoy a good hot supper.

A double guard was posted, and the prisoners were closely examined every hour to see that they did not get loose.

As darkness settled over the mesa, a lone mountain wolf set up a dreary howl from a reef far up in the buttes near the mouth of the cañon.

To some of the Rangers it sounded very suspicious, but Arnold passed it by with the remark, "Oh! that's genuine, all right. That's only the call of some she-wolf who has found a dead horse and is announcing a grand feast to all her friends."

The lonely call was answered from a cliff away over on the other side of the mesa, and the Ranger captain listened with much concern as he waited for the distant answer up in the buttes. Calling a trooper to his side he laid bare his suspicions, and they compared notes on the occurrence. He knew the country, and to the best of his ability located the warning howl as coming from the high reef on the western wall of the cañon, where high up in the cliffs and buttes a small spring known as the "Mountain Spray" made possible the site for a camp.

The answer to the warning howl came from the vicinity of the "Sleeping Cowboy Springs," so named because an Apache warrior and a young cowboy had a hand-to-hand fight at that place during the Indian raids, and though he won the fight the cowboy was found in deep sleep by his

companions, from which they could not awake
him.

These springs were in a wild, nearly inaccessi·
ble region, and altogether was a good place to
camp where water and game were plenty.

Outlaws and rustlers were still in the hills,
though they were keeping exceptionally quiet, and
the ranger knew that the continual howling was
only the warning cry of the rustler to call his pals
to arms and investigate the new camp, whose
bright fire could be seen far down the valley.

The warning notes from peak to butte soon
died away, and as the guard changed for the
night the horsemen became less suspicious, and
being in want of sleep all were soon asleep around
the camp fire, except the night watch, who,
mounted on his horse, slowly circled the camp
with his rifle ready for immediate use.

Shortly after midnight the camp was attacked,
and though the guards had kept up a vigilant
watch, they were driven in, and it looked for a
time as though the outlaws would rush the camp,
but a Ranger is a past master at bush fighting,
and so stoutly did they defend the place that the
rustlers were driven off, carrying several of their
wounded with them.

The prisoners were again tied on horseback,
and the Rangers swung to the saddle, and nearly
two hours before daybreak they left the camp and
crossed the mesa, descending to the desert through
the break in the great wall on the eastern side of
the highland.

A forced march across the desert is something
that very few would care to attempt, but Arnold

struck out across the great sand and had nearly
reached the desert station when he saw a horseman riding towards him with several mounted
men in close pursuit.

The lone rider proved to be a young Jewish
merchant, whose place had been attacked by border outlaws and looted.

There was no time for parley, so turning his
horse he rode by the side of Arnold, and all
through the running fight that was kept up for
miles he showed a degree of bravery and reckless
daring that surprised and surpassed the wild reckless Rangers themselves.

The superior workmanship of the Rangers
enabled them to kill every horse of the attacking
party, and being no match for these wild horsemen they soon surrendered.

The rustlers proved to be the party who had
attacked the camp the night before, and though
the young Jewish station keeper was badly
wounded in the shoulder he insisted on accom-
panying the officers to the jail with the prisoners.

Being nearly dead from thirst, the whole outfit
turned off of the trail at the edge of the big white
sand and rode to the "Cinco de Mayo," a small
hotel on the edge of the desert kept by an old
Mexican, Don Victorio Guellerimo De Lorma.

As they rode up to the front porch, exhausted
and covered with dust, the Ranger saw a number
of saddle horses tied near the old corral.

Arnold had dismounted and was just reaching
out to loosen the saddle cinch, when to his utter
surprise the giant form of "San Simone Dick"
loomed up on the veranda.

"You fellows don't need to indulge in any desperate fight over what trail to take," said "San Simon" as he leaned in through the door and addressed a room full of cowboys and ranchers who were busy trying to empty a big keg of whiskey.

"Here's the whole bunch out here now," and with that he turned and whipped out a big six-shooter and would have sent a bullet through the brain of the nearest outlaw if Arnold had not struck his arm and caused the bullet to go whizzing over his head.

The sound of a shot brought cowboys and ranchmen, prospectors and miners all to their feet in an instant, and all scrambled out pell mell, head over heels, through doors and windows, and for an instant it looked as though a free-for-all fight would be the result of the wild stampede; but the captain of the Rangers was a man of great resources, and removing his hat, made a speech that had the required effect upon the frenzied cattlemen and miners.

I have heard the effort repeated by an old retired army officer, Brandon Hanroohan, who as a lieutenant of cavalry led his troops in the charge at Balkalava and won a medal for bravery at Inkerman, and after giving up the army came to America and settled in the West. Though a soldier of much experience, he afterward very frankly confessed that he had never before seen or heard a man make such an able plea for law and order as this brave young Ranger made before that hardy gathering of determined ranchmen who all felt they would be doing only what was right if they avenged the death of their friends whom everyone had learned to love and respect.

It was a moment of great suspense, for the men were wild with rage, and, indeed, some of the more determined in the gathering had quietly tossed their lassoes over the rustlers' heads and were apparently waiting for the speech to be finished when they would finish the job in style.

Some were in favor of holding a trial right on the ground while others and the majority felt that they could dispense with a trial altogether.

As the young Ranger held out strongly and showed a determination not to yield and promised the ranchers that if within five days after the outlaws were landed in jail the men were not brought to trial he would capture the place with his Rangers and hang the last one in it, the cattle-men yielded and all took a big drink, swung to the saddle and rode away over the desert with the rangers towards Tombstone.

In the great sand waste they were nearly smothered by a terrible storm that blew the burning alkali dust with terrific fury; but finally towards sundown the dusty gray-looking caval-cade pulled into Tombstone, and the outlaws were all safely lodged in jail.

Much to Arnold's surprise he found that the big rumbling army stage had left town for the fork only a few hours before and was returning to the post with the troop commander, Captain MacGregor, who intended taking the field at the head of his troop to run down the outlaws.

Court convened the next day, and much to the

surprise of the people the outlaws were indicted, and though the trial dragged at times the rustlers were all convicted and hanged, and what bad men were left in the country were soon either shot or driven out.

Arnold received the thanks of all the people in the great mine and cattle region for the masterly way in which he carried out the law, and after staying in the county seat for a few days he returned to the ranch at San Simon, where he received the praise and thanks of Colonel Cornell, who felt very much the loss of his friends, "Old Ned" and "Malachite Mike," for it was through their help and good judgment he was able to make the mines the greatest producers in the world and secure for him the title of "Copper King."

The Colonel was so busy with his mines and railroads that he had no time for the ranch, and finding in Arnold a man of ability, he made him his partner in the cattle business, and the college cowboy is performing the duties of range foreman.

The Ranger had proven his worth in more ways than one, and on the invitation of a committee to send a delegation of cowboys to the great Cowboys' Riding and Roping Contest in Phoenix he not only sent a bunch of bronco busters and ropers, but went along himself, and for three days the test was in progress, and only after doing some of the finest stunts in horsemanship did his cowboys win the prize.

On the last day a great horse race was held on a level stretch out on the desert at the west of the city.

Being a free for all, there were cowboys and
Indians, soldiers and vaqueros, rangers and line
riders; all started from a line, and they were to
ride around the little mound and back again to
the starting point.

The distance was nearly three miles, and nearly
two thousand of these wild, reckless horsemen
took part in the race.

A great crowd had gathered to watch the race,
and as the loud bang of a rifle in the hands of the
starter announced that the contest was on, the
people on the hills set up a great cheer, which for
a moment drowned the terrific pounding of the
broncos' hoofs as they hammered along over the
desert, encouraged by the wild whoops and yells
of the riders as they vied with one another in giving range to the whoop that strikes terror to the
heart of the tenderfoot.

Horses fell and riders were thrown, but the
wild excitement continued, and cowboys, Indians,
vaqueros and Rangers swept on in a mad endeavor to capture the most coveted prize.

A great cloud of sand enveloped them at the
turn, but as the wind changed there rode out of
that sand cloud two horsemen who were in the
lead of all the rest, and as they drew near the goal
one could distinguish them as an American cowboy and an American Indian.

Both were mounted on powerful animals, and
as they came home together a wild yell went up
from the spectators on the hill, and the band from
the fort struck up "Dixie" and lifted every man,
woman and child of the spectators to their feet
with a frenzied whoop that mixed with the rebel

yell nearly caused the people to go mad with enthusiasm.

The Indian was a horseman, but his opponent was acknowledged to be the best in the country, and as they crossed the line the captain of the Rangers was clearly a length in the lead.

It mattered very little who won second or third, but when the winner of that wild race was announced those cowboys let a yell that could be heard for miles.

That night the cowboys departed for home, and many old-timers in the country to-day say that the cowboys' race was the greatest contest ever held among horsemen. It was the greatest gathering of wild horsemen ever held in any country, and when the call to arms was made this end of the cowboy republic sent out a bunch of cow-punchers, who, under the leadership of the king of all cowboys, whaled hell out of the best trained army of Europe and landed their valiant leader in the highest position in the land.

The cowboys and rangers returned from the great bronco-breaking contest and resumed their occupation on ranch and range.

The young Ranger captain was very much surprised upon his return to the great ranch house when Colonel Cornell handed him a letter bearing the government seal and postmarked at the Capitol.

Arnold sat on the veranda and opened the note. He read slowly word for word, then turned it around two or three times and read it again.

Then calling the Rangers, he read slowly to them the communication from the Chief Executive of this land, in which he complimented them upon the way they had enforced the law and for their noble stand in favor of law and order when besieged by a fierce mob of frenzied ranchers clamoring for the life of five cutthroats, whom among other dark deeds had murdered two harmless old miners.

That night a grand reception was held at the great rambling ranch house and the letter of commendation read as the rangers and cowboys, vaqueros and ranchmen sat at the long supper tables in the big hall room.

The Colonel made a short speech and announced to his guests that as his mining business required all of his attention and as he could make more taking money away from the Rubes in Wall Street than by raising cattle, he decided to make Arnold his manager and partner in his immense ranch holdings.

This bit of information was received with congratulations all around.

The gray-headed old judge who had fought all through the Mexican and Civil War and all the Indian Wars since Columbus landed—to hear him tell it—arose and after removing a wad of Sumatra sour dock from his face, pushed back his spectacles, shut his good eye and left the bad one open, giving him an aspect of toughness that was very much envied, stood up on a chair and started to thank the Rangers one and all for their good work in behalf of the citizens of the territory, but he had spoken very few words when he drifted and began rehearsing his own valiant deeds and modestly claimed the honor of killing every In-

dian from Massasoit down to Sitting Bull. He
would be talking yet if the cowboys hadn't
dragged him away.

After all the speeches were delivered the college cowboy sang a few college songs, much to
the delight of the "buckaroos," who looked upon
him as a hero since the wild bronco broke a hoof
against his head and never hurt him.

San Simon sang one of those breezy lays that
savor so much of the open life on the range. As
his songs have no ending he was cautioned to
stop at a sign from the Colonel.

TWO BUCKAROOS.

Two jolly buckaroos
Into civilization
Rode one day
To buy supplies
And whiskey
And go against
The faro lay.

They rode the gin mill
Through and through,
Climbed down and
Played the wheel,
Then with many a
Wild and reckless yell,
They danced the desert reel.

They danced and yelled
Throughout the night,
And were soon

All keyed up
For a grand free fight,
But they were all too full
Of the spirits of sin,
To stand any show
That fight to win.

Pretty soon their
Legs began to fail,
And the marshal
Hauled them
Away to jail.
Next morning as
They stood in line,
The Judge soaked
Each a little fine.

Those buckaroos
Rode down the trail
And cussed their
Saddest jublication
And swore by all
The sands and storms
To keep away from civilization.

Time up, "San Simon" was compelled to stop,
and though the cow-punchers would have liked to
show their approval with a wild whoop and yell,
they were afraid, for it was the first time that
many of them had sat at a table in a soft-seated
chair for years, and the white table linen and
beautiful silverware seemed to frighten them, so
they contented themselves with a few remarks and
quiet laughter at the cow-puncher's effort.

As the "buckaroos" became more accustomed to their surroundings they climbed up on the table, and sitting cross-legged like Turks, enjoyed a few draws at the ever present cigarette.

There was great fun in the cowboy singing, and as the talent had all been given a trial they started around again, and "San Simon" sang his favorite song, "The Wandering Cow-puncher."

Now I roam the dusty desert.
I'm so tough I never tire.
I eat the hairless soup dog
And drink extracts of bale wire
I have always lived so high
I expect to live a little higher.

How high I'll go I cannot tell.
If it's hotter than here, it sure is warm.
I keep a-goin' till I reach old Hell.
Up there it's cooler than this sand storm.
Compared to the desert it's not so worse,
An' I hope you'll all be there second verse.

San Simon was all aglow with enthusiasm, and the cow-punchers were all in uproarious laughter when the great south hall door swung open and in walked Captain MacGregor with a party of officers and ladies from the fort.

At the sight of the ladies there was great scrambling and dodging on the part of the cowboys who had been sprawled around the room, cowboy fashion, enjoying the wild rollicking recitations and camp songs. Some of them got down on the floor Indian fashion and watched Miss

MacGregor and the other ladies from behind chairs and table.

The actor, who had already grown big and strong, sang some of his best lays and was just winding up the first verse with—

> Now, cowboys,
> All you rally round,
> And hear my best selection,
> And if you don't
> Tear down the ranch,
> I'll sing the second section—

when the big, heavy government stage drove up in front of the ranch house and the dusty driver threw down a box marked "Headquarters Camp, Arizona Rangers, San Simon Ranch, via Fort Huachuca, Arizona."

Only a few men left the hall when the stage drove up, but those few were Rangers, and they took the box and dragged it around by the smoke house, where Arnold broke it open and took out a beautiful cowboy saddle, bridle sturs and lasso.

With broad grinning faces the rangers bore the saddle and trappings to the ranch house and to the surprise and wonder of all the cowboys and ranchmen Arnold walked to the raised platform, where stood the piano, and mounting, made a short speech as he held saddle and all up to the gaze of the gawking spectators.

In his speech he noted how the Chief Executive had expressed his admiration for the Rangers and cowboys and commended them for their bravery and manly qualities, and in appreciation

the cowboys and rangers had purchased the finest
saddle that could be bought in the territory and
were going to send it on to Washington to the
only cowpuncher who ever became President.

This part of the speech was listened to with
pent-up enthusiasm by the vaqueros, who, owing
to the presence of ladies, were too timid to yell.
They listened attentively until Arnold read the
inscription worked in silver on the back of the
saddle seat, "To the King of all Cowboys, from
the Arizona Rangers."

As he finished, Miss MacGregor, who had been
behind him, reached up and pulled a curtain from
over a picture that hung on the wall above the
piano.

The picture was one she drew that day. It was
no great work of art, and if it was the cow-
punchers wouldn't know the difference, but as
that curtain was drawn aside, there hung the
picture of their patron saint, "The King of all
Cowboys," with his big white teeth, his eye-
glasses, and a big slouch hat jammed over on the
side of his head. The wild war-whoop that went
up from that bunch of horsemen nearly lifted the
roof. They whooped and yelled, rode each other
around, pitching and bucking like wild broncos
and for a time Colonel Cornell thought they
would tear down the whole ranch.

With great difficulty quiet was resumed and
the saddle smuggled out of the room into the
smoke-house, where it was packed and sent on to
Washington.

In due time a note came back announcing its
arrival and inviting all the cowpunchers to a

grand swauree and round-up to be held at the
Capitol along in March, when he was to be for-
mally installed as foreman for the U. S. brand.

As the time for the big rodero at Washington
drew near the cowboys and rangers, roughriders
and ranchmen departed with their broncos for the
grand swauree to be held at the United States
outfits headquarter's ranch.

Everything was done in true cowboy style and
the "King of all Cowboys" was made President
of the United States.

I visited the post one day and Miss MacGregor
read for my edification a few lines from a letter
Arnold had written from the Capitol. Though I
could not get my eye on the greeting or ending
of the epistle it must have been of great import
to the young lady, for she guarded it very closely
and shaded it cleverly while she read: "The
natives here are all a queer looking outfit. Most
of them wear their Sunday clothes and look like
rich gamblers and faro-dealers one sees around
Bisbee and Tombstone. I attended a lecture last
night and heard the eloquent Chauncey deliver
one of his best orations. When he threw out a
few bouquets to the cowboys, 'San Simon' nearly
jumped through the roof, and the fellows all
'lowed he'd be a winning bet at a camp-meeting.
We all supposed he'd storm and rear out onto the
platform, lay his guns on the table, roll up his
pants legs, unbutton his flannel shirt, spit on his
hands, shove his hat over on the side of his head
and emphasizing his remarks with a heavy fist,
now and then stopping to see if anyone wanted to

fight like 'Mustang Mike' used to do when making a speech in old Hankin's trading post.

"Nothing of the kind. He was a tall, smooth-looking man, dressed in black with about two acres of white shirt front and a collar high enough to fence a mellon patch. He waltzed out gently and delivered a neat little speech, in which he said it was his ambition when young to be a pirate or cowboy. He looked more like the chaplain at the fort than a pirate.

"We all are having a fine time. The trails here are all straight and wide. We busted a few broncos and lassoed the big policemen and in other ways covered ourselves with glory.

"I saw the fire engines making a run the other day. It certainly was grand and beats the old 'Cloudburst Fire Company' of Tombstone all hollow. 'San Simon' was in jail the other night. He says it's a fine place and beats being tied up to the wheel of a freight wagon.

"I used to think Rawhide Manor upon Mescal Heights was the limit of architectural endeavor, but there's buildings here in this city that can beat it easy.

"We have all been living in a hotel like civilized folks, but some of the fellows got lonesome and moved out into the corrals and wagon yards, where they could sleep more comfortable and homelike. We got pretty good grub and of course we put on our best manners while eating.

"The fellows all have learned to sit in chairs at the table and don't talk loud or swear any more.

"The women here paint their heads yellow and

they all are about the usual age of women at this
time of the year."

That's all I heard of that letter, and the rest
must be very important, for though I was ten feet
away, she held it very securely and when she was
done reading she stowed it away carefully in her
bosom.

CHAPTER XVI.

SOCIETY IN THE BONANZA CIRCLE.

AFTER the grand swauree in Washington was ended the cowboys all returned home, and shortly after, much to my surprise, I received an invitation to attend a grand reception at the big ranchhouse in honor of the ranger and his wife, formerly Miss MacGregor. It certainly was a grand affair and Colonel Cornell announced that Arnold would have full charge of all his immense land and cattle interests in the southwest, and also in Mexico.

Miss MacGregor looked charming and many a young officer and ranchman departed that night with a heavy heart, for this beautiful young lady had been the hope and admiration of all the young blades around the country.

Everything was booming in the great bonanza circle and millions of dollars were invested in the Bisbee basin.

Many disputes arose over mining claims and Arnold found it necessary to go to the basin to preserve order. He had already handed in his resignation, but it would not be accepted until order and quiet had been restored in the great mineral district.

The ranger had little difficulty in restoring peace and the disputants laid away their guns and fought it out in the land courts.

While in town the ranger was the recipient of many well wishes from the host of old friends who welcomed him back.

Arnold, or the Ranger, as his friends preferred to call him, was given a big reception by the miners and prospectors, who greatly admired his manly qualities.

Old Dutch Baker, who had peddled his claims for a million, gave him a ride in his coupé. The carriage was new and very costly and the horses in their silver mounted harnesses would outshine anything in the swell Eastern cities. Old Dutch was no society man, but he was always in style and on the doors of the carriage was the wolly old miner's coat of arms, emblazoned in bold relief so that all might see—a pick and shovel crossed on a pack saddle.

"Pine-tree Bill" filled the august position of coachman and being a hard drinker he generally gave good satisfaction to his employer. "Pine-tree" got his name from the fact that one of his legs had been chopped off by an Apache Indian, and he ever since wore a pine stump to faciliate navigation.

As a study in rags old "Pine-tree" was a work of art and old Dutch would take first money at any tramp show.

Don't think for a moment it was a lack of funds that caused them to go about in such clothes, but to keep in tone with the general surroundings, and it was, as Old Dutch used to say, "Art for art's sake."

Sometimes when they were drunk and the horses started to run away, why they just let them run and stop when they got ready. Old Dutch had drowned his wooden shoes in the North Sea, and was altogether a good citizen.

The crust of society is sometimes like the top layer of a mud pie and very often a man will spend the smaller part of a million on his friends over the bar, but would not give him ten cents to save his life. Old Baker never came under that category and any miner in the basin could say he was liberal to a fault.

The grizzly old gold digger was born some days before yesterday and could tell a man when he saw one. If a man with a twenty-two calibre head on a forty-five frame should come along it would take old Dutch a very short time to gauge his standing. He always walked with a slow, swinging stride until some months ago, when some cowboys goosed him, and since then he moves along with a quick, nervous, switching gait.

Being an old timer, a relic of the days when the Apaches used to waltz up and down the desert, trimming out the settlers so that there were not enough ranchers left in the San Simon Valley to constitute a quorum for the transaction of business after Geronimo and his painted boys made a raid through the place, he was always ready to thrash out a little local history.

At the reception that night the Ranger made a

speech and acquitted himself favorably as be-
fitted a man who had been to see the President.

Most all the old timers did a turn, and among
the new lights was a "Cousin Jack," who recited
a poem entitled,

"A TEN DAY MINER."

Ah! dam we ould tuss,
Think lad I'm daffy?
Sit easy lad, no fuss.
Touch pipe a bit ould son,
Ten days work's nuf f'ra mon,
Hist one Jack then on—mov' on.

This easy life's nuf f'r us,
Pipe, drink, a wee bit tuss,
Shake leg at dance,
Now an' then fuss,
I say you,—mov' on.
No! No boss f'r Jawn,
What's a ten-day mon?

Two years in Butte,
Three thousand bucks,
Some faro bank,
Some whiskey drank,
Some gin-mill fuss,
A little wine,
A wee bit tuss.
Well, no use t' squak,
If I had a bike—
But it's walk! Walk!
You dam fool, you walk.

If I had a bike—
But hike! hike! hike!
You leather headed fool you,
Now you hike! hike! hike!
Three years in mine,
Short stroll down line,
Then—oh! You fool—well—
The best place f'r you's in hell.

"I've felt just that way after pay-day," said an
old miner, just in from Tonapah, and many another could have said the same had he cared to.

"Bay State Bill" recited a little verse and won
the hearts of all who had ever lived in the hills
of the old homestead.

I met a lass
In the Berkshire hills,
While strolling
Along the lea.

Her face so fair,
Her golden hair,
And eyes like the
Deep blue sea.
Completely won my
Wild young heart,
And took the
Breath from me.

She tripped along,
And left no trail,
Like an angel
In ecstasy.

Apologizing to
The world at large,
She was pretty
And lovely to see,
But she never
Smiled on my
Pleading gaze,
So the devil a word
I said to her,
And she said
The same to me.

This effort was marred somewhat by a tall, slim looking colored man who came tearing into the hall and rushing up to Arnold, began in his Southern jargon, "Mr. Cap'n of de Rangers, I presents mah sef teh y'u, most gran' lookin' pussonage, teh tell y'u dat a dispute as took place at a cullud dance what was ended with a big stab. De big yaller nigger draw'd a razzor outen his clo's an' fust dat nigger he killed his self den de odder nigger he killed his self, den he killed a woman Chinaman. 'Clare I can't tell 'zactly where it did happen. But y'u foller that thar road as w'at y'u fust comes to den y'u bears off a little an' goes up the next road. Then down two roads an' over a' nudder road. Den 'cross some more roads, an' keep agoin' till y'u comes teh de place as whare a dance is if daze dare yet an' dem's de niggers as wat done de killin'.'"

That coon was so excited that the officers had to lock him up until morning, though the knife marks on his head and clothes bore out the statement that he had been at a party and some one had used a razor on him in a social way.

Old "Hot Foot Cal" read a little essay on the wandering miner. Here is what little I heard of it, for I must say the commotion was something terrible, even to an editor accustomed to stormy scenes:

"THE WANDERING MINER, BY "HOT FOOT CAL."

"Ah! dam me. I've alluz been unlucky—had I stayed one hour longer in South Africa I'da' found the biggest diamond in the world, an' like a bloody fool I peddled me claims in Nome an' mushed out iv th' dam country just when me pard struck it rich, an' it wuz th' same in Colgardie.

"A dam ornery mule fell off a mountain with me in Peru an' I wuz laid up in th' horspital fur six months with a spraint back, but I'da' sure made it in th' Yaqui country if th' dam Indians hadn't tried to comb my hair with an axe.

"Not that I'm a poor manger pal, but it's th' lucks what's agin me. Here I stakes me last dollar on a chicken ranch out in th' 'San Simon' Valley, an' th' dam coyotes steals th' last dirty one uv um.

"Wuz timberin' a shaft out in th' Huachucas an' mist me footin' un nearly bus' me head when I stumpled eight sets. Had th' nawmawnya in Butte an' had t' drag it. Now th' dam sand blows like hell in a man's face—yeh think I'll stay in this dam place?—In a pig's valise I will. Soon as th' first train goes I go. What th' juz a man want t' spend his life in one place for?

"Frisco's me next town. I may go on up into Idaho, or p'haps I'll take ship t' China, but I'll go t' hell if I stay here.

"Bloody good place t' work—th' hell you say.

Ah, tell that to him as what's a bum. Me work in a mine again. I'd see yuh in hell first."

Old "Hot Foot" retired, followed by calls of "Good boy," "Give 'em th' other barrel," "Twist 'es tail," "Spur 'em along from belly to back," "Claw hell out of 'em old man," and a few other words of encouragement I fail to recall.

Colonel Bob Slauter, at one time sheriff of the county, made a little speech on social problems. Not being in very good voice he cut his talk a little short, but being the sheriff, what he said went a long way.

"While filling the office of sheriff my conscience never bothered me very much on the question of hanging. None of my prisoners were tame enough to hang—they were all shot or died with their boots on, though many managed to fly the country. I must say that the clear, dry air of this wild solitude seems to put the very devil into the people who live here and woe to the poor devil who tries to fill the sheriff's office, which is, I believe, more dangerous than running a newspaper and criticizing these self-same devils. What we need here in this end of Arizona is a modern graveyard, not that anyone is dead, but just to be in fashion.

"Nobody around here is sufficiently self-sacrificing to croak, and the dry air is so bracing that those who get hung won't stay dead. That's just why we want the graveyard and to be in style.

"Just think of it. Burying a man up in a cottonwood tree with a forty-foot rope around his neck to hold him there. Why, that's shocking.

"I must say things have taken a change for the

better and the settlers are all quiet and tame.
You all know that the average settler in Arizona
is gentle and smart and as a linguist he can't be
beat. He speaks very fluently Spanish, Dutch,
Apache, Yaqui, Irish, Missouri, the sign language, can swear by the International Code, and
when it comes to talking 'Cousin Jack,' Berkshire
Hills, or plain English, he can't be beat."

Those few words of praise won that ex-sheriff
a howl of applause that plainly showed they were
all right in place and stamped him as a speaker.

For the special edification of a party of Eastern
mining men old "Stud Hoss Joe" recited that
little cowboy sketch which every tenderfoot has
to listen to when he is turned loose among the
cowpunchers for the first time.

Here it is. Lean back and get ready:

"Tenderfoot look on me. I'm a he-horned
devil from Bitter Creek—up yonder whar she
forks—I drags these mountains out o' place, fight
Injuns an' eats live wild cats. I massacres
dragoons, claws up hell-fire an' coughs like a
volcano. Mountain oysters fills my belly an' I
lathers my face with red-hot lead when I goes to
shave. I sleeps with rattlesnakes, centipedes an'
tarantalus an' totes as pocket pieces, live Gila
monsters. I'm a wolf, an' it's my time to howl;
a buckin' bronco an' it's my time to leap; a roarin'
lion an' it's my privelage to claw up old hell. So
come on you limb of the devil an' bring me needle
an' thread for to sew up the hole in the back of
my breeches."

Some of those men nearly died with laughter,

and old "Stud Hoss" Joe was the hero of the
whole outfit.

Old "Humpback Clancy" viewed the proceedings from the outside. And as he cautiously
gazed through the window it could be plainly seen
that he was mounted on a fleet footed mule, and
evidently fully prepared to take flight at the first
sign of danger.

"Old Musty Mulligan" was the next on the
programme. He played an obligato on the fiddle
and here is what the musical critics of the "Bisbee
Daily Dynamiter" had to say about his playing :

"Señor Mulligan scored a great hit at the 'Social' held in the Miners' Hall last night, when he
played the fiddle in E flat, almost giving to the
violin the tenderness of a human voice. He
played the Concerto in B minor of Anheuser-
Busch, and its revelations of a strange new beauty
were prepetual. There was no cessation of dis-
coveries in the violinist's work. It was delicate
and learned, grave and extremely sensitive. It
had the faculty of being ever new and captivat-
ing. He played a concerto by 'Cave Creek
George,' and it was as if it had never been played
before and as he changed legs and rosined up his
fiddle the audience broke out in irrepressible applause which they kept up with great ardor until
the old man, carried away by the enthusiasm,
busted his G string.

"After replacing the broken string with a piece
of bale wire, he flew at it again and was compelled
to saw out a new tune each time he was recalled.
Being nearly winded he came on the last time
dragging old 'Fryin' Pan' to the front with him

to share the honors, for it was 'Fryin' Pan' who made that fiddle."

The Mormon Elder with a twenty-four knot marriage record, sang a few songs. I would not say a good word for him if I could. He was the biggest liar that ever lived, for the lies that I told him he turned right around and told them back to me again.

Well, he pulled his freight and then a "Rube," a big wart on the face of humanity, came forth and tickled the floor with a broom, for the Highland Fling was next.

Prof. Douglas Wallace delivered a neat little lecture and though he was somewhat past the allotted three-score years and ten, his feet had no respect for the long white hair on the venerable head when the pipers struck up that brave Scotch tune that thrills the heart of every true son of Scotland.

In perfect time to the "blaws" and swirls of the wild Scotch music the venerable old gentleman executed every whirl and swing of the Highland fling, and had every spectator in the house cheering like mad.

Every heart beat wildly, and as quiet could not be restored the meeting was brought to an end and the people departed.

As Arnold was retiring to his room at the Castle Rock Inn, he met "San Simon Dick, who had just arrived after a dangerous trip across the "sands."

"How's everything in the Basin?" inquired San Simon.

"Sliding along easy," replied the Ranger in his usual Southern drawl.

"Going to stop with me to-night?" the Ranger asked.

"No," slowly replied San Simon. "You see, I pilled down on the desert last night, so I'm not sleepy. 'Sides, I think I'll pay my respects to the hog ranch. Met a squaw out on the desert and thought I'd make it, but when she saw me coming, she got down and began to paw sand, so I guess I'll go up and help round up some heifers."

The men parted for the night, and the next morning Arnold was called on to arrest the negro who had done all the carving at the colored dance that night.

He had no difficulty in locking up the murderer, and noticing a crowd hanging around he dropped into the office of the Justice of the Peace just in time to hear the verdict rendered by the coroner's jury after they had viewed the bodies found out at the scene of the nigger dance.

The verdict: "We, the jury, after plowing our way through a sand storm and viewing these carved-up remains of a Chinee and some niggers, do find that these dead men and any other dead men who may be found around the place, came to their deaths in a manner to us unknown, and what's more, we don't give a dam.

Signed: "Colonel Billy Plaster,
"Foreman of all juries that sits on dead men."

When the jury was dismissed they repaired to the saloon known as "The Battered Eye," where the windows were decorated in bold letters with this bit of advice, "If drink interferes with your business, why, quit your business."

After a few rounds of drinks with a toast now and then, such as,

S'lute your pardners,
An' treat 'em well,
Fly 'round th' corners,
Like a bat out o' hell,

or by way of variation to the usual "here's now" or "here's lookin' at yuh," with the answer of "go to it" or "fill yer tank," some bright light wo' sing out,

"Here's to the sands,
And the lizard lands,
And the lass
Who lives alone,
And the maidens fair,
Who live up there,
At the ranch
Of the old dry bones."

After drinking around a few times and nearly talking each other to death, they all separated and waltzed away about their business.

Being near the noon hour, Arnold and a friend took lunch at the "Pick and Shovel" restaurant.

The Ranger slowly asked his friend what he would have, and as he gave his order in the usual Southern tone to the waitress, "Mustang Mattie" turned on her heel and yelled in response to his order of bacon and eggs with a small piece of steak, toast and coffee, "Copper the Jack, play the ace high, put wings on the hog, sicken the loaf, an' draw one in Java."

A fellow did not have to wait very long here

to be served with a meal. "Mustang Mattie," ably assisted by "Creole Kate," "Swanee Sue" and "Sandstorm Sal," kept the pot boiling and grub was continually flying t'.rough the air from all directions.

The meal finished, the Ranger and his friend paid their four bits and walked down the narrow street.

They had hardly , walked ten yards when the Ranger's bright eye caught a glimpse of the shaggy looking form of old Kelly emerging from the portals of the "Pig's Ear Cafe," one door up from the "Dynamite Saloon."

The old scout shaded his eyes and surveyed them closely as they approached.

"There are two of yeh, says the devil to his horns," came from the scout as he advanced slowly with outstretched hand for a friendly shake.

Arnold shook the big rough hand very warmly and listened to the old scout's words of praise with great pleasure, for old Kelly very seldom used words of praise on anyone and never before on him.

"Kid, yer 'iv done fine. Ye sprize me. Whar'iv I been? Oh! down in the Yaqui country on a camel hunt. I just come in across the 'big sand.' Lad that's a terrible trip," continued the scout. "Don't yez ever try to cross the desert. Go 'round by way of hell. It's much cooler and not half so dusty. I nearly got lost over on Sow-belly Creek the day before three o'clock yesterday, but I managed to pull through.

"Kid, a time was as when I could whale hell out of you."

"Well, if you should try now," replied the Ranger, laughing, "you might be like the fellow who picked up a wild cat and couldn't turn him loose."

"Right ye are," answered Kelly, and tipping his hat over on the back of his head and rubbing his hands on his face, he drawled out, "Let's take a swashay over to the 'Paradise Lost' undertaking parlors and have a look at them niggers. If festifications sets in we can't congeal after looking at them stiffs, so we'd better go early."

Arnold declined and so they stood around and old Kelly told of the wonderful shooting to be had up on the Cimmeron and over in the Petrified fortsts and along the Great Cañon.

After a few more long winded yarns on hunting in the Cañon de Chelley and S. H. mountains, the men separated, Kelly to inspect the gin-mills, and Arnold and his friend returned to the Castle Rock Inn.

Everything was quiet in the Basin. The vigilance committee was so crooked that it went into voluntary liquidation, so one-half could avoid hanging the other. A few men have expired as the result of careless handling of guns in other men's hands, but the Rangers have kept the toughs out and the country now is as quiet as a town in the Berkshire Hills. Of course, the region still has a touch of wildness, and in fact, the only tame animal in these parts is the friendly gray-back, but as a general thing the "big sand" is as orderly as any other open country.

The whole Southwest is on the jump.

Colonel Cornell has mines and railroads scattered all over the great mineral plateau.

Arnold has resigned from the Rangers and from his beautiful home at the "big ranch" looks after the Colonel's immense cattle interests.

The last time I was at the "Dripping Springs" Ranch, I had lunch with the Ranger and his charming wife and family.

Prof. Smith is chief engineer for the mining company, and the actor, the college cowboy and all the rest of the outfit are enjoying life and building up the new country.

"San Simon Dick" fought through the Yaqui war and stole a maiden from the Indians.

Here is the story as written by the Ranger's wife, and handed to me.

That lady being of great culture and well versed in the music and melody of romantic expression, has told the story in a way I think is certainly charming and away ahead of any effort of the poet laureate of "Lone Dog Hill," who turns out more stuff in one week than would patch hell a mile.

Now believe me, that's going some, for the sky pilot up in the lookout at the meeting-house was in the habit of quoting from the works of this woolly old poet nearly every Sunday. All the cowpunchers and miners voted him to be the best mixer of rhyme in the world.

CHAPTER XVII.

LOVE AND WAR.

THE soft silvery glow of the tropical moonlight faded away as the balmy breezes stirred by the life and the light as the last lingering trace of the long, long night disappeared, when the deep dazzling lines in the east told the slumbering souls that day was dawning.

Silently the children of the sun arose and facing the east with hands uplifted to heaven as if in supplication to the Sun-God to forgive them their sins, they chanted their simple prayer.

The sun rose slowly over the horizon, painting the soft southern sky a brilliant color of gold, while its rich radiant rays kissed the tips of the peaks of the wild rugged range whose buttes and mountain tops seemed to reach far up into the heavens and doubly reflecting their magnificent grandeur in the clear, cool lakes and rippling waters in the, valley far, far below where the silvery scintillation of the shadowy waters' shimmering surface made it seem like a garden enchanted.

In this valley so lovely and verdant, where violets were always visible through the veil of wild rose vines which when lost in the lilies that lined the lagoons and lent light to the colors contrasted, could still by their tropical essence be traced in the tangle of redolent roses mingled in the mild mellow bloom of bright orange blossoms, sweet scented jessamine and beautiful, frail, fragrant flora in this fair, fertile land of wild flowers with its lucious fruits of wonderful color and flavor.

For many moons no cloud ever crossed that silvery sky and the soft salient sunlight in the sweet scented solitude where no noise ever severed the silence sublime, made it seem like a place for the seraphs to soar over its acres of orchids and lilies.

In this placid peaceful place all was sacred and sublime. Here the Sun-Gods ruled supreme. Beneath this southern sunlight's soft and searching glow all nature seemed to smile on this fair land, reflecting all its grandeur in the lakes and silvery waters, seemed to change the verdant valleys with their wondrous mighty mountains to the mystery of the measureless mirage.

In this morass and tangled jungle of wild flowers of wondrous colors, with its climate like a sunny day in June, great towering pyramids and mighty temples strewn in wondrous tumbled ruins told a tale of deep devotion of the children of the Sun.

Not since Spanish pride profaned it have they trod this sacred vale, in this glorious garden of the gods. To the west, and near the gravestones, stood the monument of Tolto-moc-chi. Here it stood for longer ages than is told in the tribe's tradition.

Lost at the base in a world of ferns and flowers
with a single wreath of wild jessamine, the sacred
flower of the Yaqui climbing to its top from the
tangle of tropical verdure below.

Down through this beautiful valley flowed the
"El Rio de Yaqui," a wild, roaring torrent that
stormed along through the deep and forbidding
cañons in the mountains until emerging through
the trough in the great mountain wall where the
buttes and foot hills break on the savannas and
seeming to sink in the soft rich soil it sifted itself
silently through the thick tangle of tropical verdure, here and there tranquilly gathering to form
the limpid lakes that listlessly lay in the valley and
pictured the precipices that lined their shores as
the spectral shadows gave features fantastic to the
sun gods carved in bold relief upon the cliffs as
they gazed out over the glossy bosom of the
sacred waters of this lovely solitude—sublime in
its silence and stillness.

These temples and palaces in this sacred garden
of the gods were ruthlessly sacked and plundered
by the cruel Spanish conquerors, who murdered
the Indian chief and tried to enslave his brave
warriors.

The Indians retreated into the almost inaccessable mountain peaks and gathering their scattered
forces marched down from the mesa and hid in
the morasses until the silence of night had settled
in the valley.

Then in that night so dark it seemed all light
had left the world, they stole out upon the unsuspecting enemy and killed everything that con-
tained life in the invaders' camp.

The bodies were dragged away and thrown into the volcanoes to appease the wrath of the God
of War.

The Indians vowed never to set foot in the
sacred vale until the return of the sun-god.   So
they jealously guarded the evergreen gardens of
the gods and patiently awaited the return of their
chief, who every day passed over them and gave
life and light to all the world.

In the highest mountain peaks they built a
temple and from its altars offering prayers to their
long lost chief in heaven, who though he continued to smile on them still held his course and
not a word has he spoken in answer to their
pleadings as the high priest lowly whispered, at
the sunrise every morning, "To his eloquence let
us listen."

Gold was found in many places along those silvery streams and rivers.   Rich quartz ledges
pitted out along the cliffs.

All were jealously guarded by the chiefs and
high priests, who forbade any strangers to enter
their domain.

The wandering gold hunters were killed or
driven out of the forbidden El Dorado and Mexican troops were sent to open the great bonanzas.

In the fierce Indian wars that followed the
Yaqui braves fought desperately and repeatedly
defeated the government troops.   They swarmed
over the border and exchanged their gold for
high power rapid-firing rifles at the isolated
trading posts and lonely stations in the Arizona
desert.

General Torras with his wild and reckless

vaqueros was repeatedly beaten and his cavalry scattered.

Evidently the Indians were led by a man of great military ability, for they fought together, cut off convoys, captured pack trains, drove back the soldiers and laid waste the whole country from the great American desert on the north to the fever swamps on the south, and from the Sierra Madras on the east to the Pacific Ocean on the west.

They fought with a fanatical fierceness and reckless daring that nothing could check, but through all their wild raids and fierce charges the genius of some bold and skillful leader could plainly be seen in the well planned and concentrated attacks.

The Mexican Government offered a substantial reward for the arrest of a young girl known as Santa Teresa, who seemed to have great influence among the Indians, who worshipped her as the daughter of the Sun. For the priests had read it plainly on the great Aczetic calendar how the people were to be led by a maiden whose skill and ability would enable them to drive the hated intruders over the great mountain wall into the ocean, and restore their fallen cities and ruined temples and prepare the country for the return of their gods.

Santa Teresa had long lived among the Indians at Magdalena, where her father kept a trading store. Her mother, an American lady, died when she was young and to provide for her careful training she was sent to the old mission San

Xavier in the quaint and ancient city in the Arizona desert, where under the watchful eyes of the
sisters she received a thorough education, after
the manner obtaining in the States.

While living in this quaint and ancient city she
had often attended the great cowboy carnivals
held every fall after the great rodero had been
finished.

Among those wild and reckless horsemen there
was one who caught her fancy. A lad whose
skill and reckless riding won him nearly every
prize. Tall and lithesome, true and manly, this
stalwart young giant was crowned king of all the
cowboys by the cattlemen who had gathered from
the range.

This blond-haired, blue-eyed giant, whose
glowing adolescence brought forth words of adul-
tation as she sat and framed her fancies in fervid
lonesome longing for his love and life's fruitition,
roamed the range along the frontier, knew the
springs and feeding places on all the plains down
in Sonora and from his ranch out in the San
Simon he had often crossed th. border on a visit
to this maiden, whose lustrious eyes of languid
blackness and whose rare and radiant features
had completely won his heart.

The blood-haired chief, San Simon, had defeated all the soldiers whom Diaz had sent against
him, and by reckless, able daring won a place high
in the councils of the fierce and warlike Yaquis,
who looked upon this daring leader as one sent
to them from heaven by the sun-god whom they
worshipped.

San Simon fell ill of fever and was nursed by this fair princess until he had fully gained his strength.

Then he was loath to leave the maiden who had won his heart completely. When the braves divined the reason they were wild with rage and anger at this profanation of their princess, the daughter of the Sun.

When they saw that they were lovers they were taken to the temple and the chiefs in sober council solemnly assembled, sentenced them to suffer death.

That night a friend released them and together they departed for his home across the border. Wild with rage the warriors pursued them, but in that night of awful darkness they together, all undaunted, left the wild and rugged mountains and descended to the valley.

There they traveled through the flowers; through the orchids and the lilies; through the daisies, all delicious in the drippings of the dew where the misty veil hung densely in the dells.

In this romantic rural place with its magnolias and mignonettes, all the flowers so melliferous in their wildest profusion sending forth their sweetly flowing flavors made this wonderful luxuriant florescence seem like the abode of mammon.

In this strange romantic place they roamed as if in esctacy, enchanted as the sun-god in solstice smiled on this fair scene seraphic.

They wandered along by the wild weeping willows where the wide spreading stream reflected their shadows and the wind from the woods

seemed to spread the mist on the meadows and
soften the scene so it looked like a shadow of
heaven and seeming so much like a dream that the
wanderers in bewilderment wondered while the
sunlight in shaping the shadows covered the
spectral sepulchre where the souls leave all sorrow
and sadness and live in the light of a long, long
dream, where the dreaming is something the
saints all live and not seeming as they seemed to
seem.

Then they turned and journeyed homeward,
crossed the buttes and rugged mountains, crossed
the trails and raging rivers till they struck the
friendly frontier, where the border line divides
them from the children of the sun.

As they crossed the friendly border they could
see the priests pursuing, but they never stopped
to listen, and kept pressing towards the frontier
as the sun was slowly setting in the silvery clouds
of evening.

There the priests in rage beheld them and in
wildest supplication begged the sun-god stop their
flight.

But he heeded not their pleadings and slowly
sank behind the great mountain reef into his bed
of blue in the glossy bosom of the placid Pacific.

The southwinds moaned through the cliffs and
cañons. A great storm swept in from the solitude and breaking in terrific fury against the
great western mountain wall left the country in
silence and alone.

That night as the last golden gleam of the south
sea sunset was lost in the gloom of the southern

cross and the soft silvery twilight tranquilly gathered in the gloom these lovers vowed forever to be
one. As in the days gone by and in the days to
come.

THE END.

LaVergne, TN USA
20 May 2010

183419LV00003B/52/P

9 781120 236319